FLASHMAPS
SAN FRANCISCO

D0981550

Editor
Steven K. Amsterdam

Creative Director
Fabrizio La Rocca

Cartographer
David Lindroth

Designer
Tigist Getachew

Editorial Contributors
Jennifer Brewer
Martha Schulman

Cartographic Contributors
Edward Faherty
Sheila Levin
Page Lindroth
Marcy S. Pritchard
Eric Rudolph

Special Sales

Fodor's Travel Publications are available at special discounts for bulk purchases for sales promotions or premiums. Special editions, including personalized covers, excerpts of existing guides, and corporate imprints, can be created in large quantities for special needs. For more information, contact your local bookseller or write to Special Markets, Fodor's Travel Publications, 201 East 50th St., New York, NY 10022. Inquiries from Canada should be directed to your local Canadian bookseller or sent to Random House of Canada, Ltd., Marketing Dept., 2775 Matheson Blvd. East, Mississauga, Ontario L4W4P7. Inquiries from the United Kingdom should be sent to Fodor's Travel Publications, 20 Vauxhall Bridge Rd., London, England SW1V 2SA. **ISBN 0-679-00009-7**

PRINTED IN THE UNITED STATES OF AMERICA 10 9 8 7 6 5 4 3 2 1

Area Codes: All (415) unless otherwise noted.

EMERGENCIES

Ambulance/Fire/Police ☎ 911

American Red Cross ☎ 202-0600

Abducted, Abused and Exploited Children ☎ 800/248-8020

Burn Center ☎ 353-6255

Boys Town National Hotline ☎ 800/448-3000

Child Crisis Service ☎ 695-5195

Crisis Line for the Handicapped ☎ 800/426-4263

Drug Crisis Line ☎ 362-3400

Missing Children Hotline ☎ 800/222-3463

National Runaway Switchboard ☎ 800/621-4000

Poison Control Information ☎ 800/523-2222

Rape Crisis Line ☎ 647-7273

Rape Treatment Center ☎ 821-3222

San Francisco AIDS Hotline ☎ 863-AIDS

San Francisco General Hospital ☎ 206-8000

Suicide Prevention ☎ 781-0500

T.A.L.K. Line for Parents Under Stress ☎ 441-5437

Toxic Chemical and Oil Spills ☎ 800/424-8802

U.S. Marshals Service ☎ 436-7677

Westside Crisis Services ☎ 353-5055

Youth Crisis Hotline ☎ 800/448-4663

ENTERTAINMENT

BASS Tickets ☎ 510/762-2277

BASS Tickets Performing Arts Line ☎ 776-1999

Cal Performances ☎ 510/642-9988

City Box Office ☎ 392-4400

Downtown Center Box Office ☎ 775-2021

MovieLine ☎ 777-FILM

San Francisco Ballet ☎ 703-9400

San Francisco Film Society ☎ 931-3456

San Francisco Opera ☎ 864-3330

San Francisco Symphony ☎ 431-5400

TIX Bay Area ☎ 433-7827

SERVICES

AAA ☎ 800/222-4357

Black Women's Resource Center ☎ 510/763-9501

California Office of Tourism ☎ 800/862-2543

Center For Independent Living ☎ 863-0581

Lesbian/Gay/Bi-Sexual Communities United Against Violence ☎ 333-4357

Mission Cultural Center ☎ 821-1155

National Parks ☎ 556-0561

National Weather Service ☎ 364-7974

Native American Health Center ☎ 621-8051

Oakland Convention and Visitors Authority ☎ 510/839-9000

Planned Parenthood ☎ 441-5454

Redwood Empire Assoc. Visitor Info Center ☎ 394-5991

San Francisco AIDS Foundation ☎ 487-3000

San Francisco Convention & Visitors Bureau ☎ 974-6900

San Francisco Dept. of Public Health ☎ 554-2500

State Parks ☎ 330-6300

Time of Day ☎ 767-8900

US Postal Service ☎ 800/275-8777

Women's Building ☎ 431-1180

Visitor Information Center ☎ 391-2000; 391-2001

SPECTATOR SPORTS

BASS Tickets ☎ 510/762-2277

Cow Palace ☎ 469-6065

3Com Park/Giants Tickets ☎ 467-8000

49ers Tickets ☎ 468-2249

Golden State Warriors Tickets ☎ 510/986-2200

Oakland A's Tickets ☎ 510/638-0500

Oakland Coliseum ☎ 510/639-7700

Oakland Raiders ☎ 800/949-2626

San Jose Sharks ☎ 408/287-4275

Stanford Sports ☎ 800/BEAT-CAL

U.C. Berkeley Sports ☎ 800/GO-BEARS

Area Codes: All (415) unless otherwise noted.

TRANSPORTATION

AC Transit ☎ 510/817-1717

Amtrak ☎ 800/872-7245

BART ☎ 992-2278; 510/465-2278

Blue and Gold Fleet ☎ 773-1188

CalTrain ☎ 800/660-4287

Golden Gate Ferry ☎ 923-2000

Golden Gate Transit ☎ 923-2000

Green Tortoise ☎ 821-0803

Greyhound ☎ 800/231-2222

Greyhound Terminal ☎ 495-1569

Harbor Bay Ferry ☎ 510/769-5500

MUNI ☎ 673-6864

Oakland/Alameda Ferry
☎ 510/522-3300

Oakland International Airport
☎ 510/577-4000

Pier 39 ☎ 981-7437

Red and White Fleet ☎ 800/229-2784

SamTrans ☎ 800/660-4287

San Francisco International Airport
☎ 876-7809

San Jose International Airport
☎ 408/277-4759

SFO Airporter, Airport Shuttle
☎ 495-8404

SFO Rides—Airport Transit Hotline
☎ 800/736-2008

Super Shuttle ☎ 558-8500

TravInfo Hotline ☎ 817-1717;
650/817-1717, 408/817-1717,
510/817-1717

Veteran's Cab ☎ 552-1300

PARKS AND RECREATION

Airtime San Francisco ☎ 759-1177

Bay to Breakers Race ☎ 512-5000

Berkeley Iceland ☎ 510/843-8800

East Bay Regional Parks District
☎ 510/635-0135

Golden Gate Park Golf Course
☎ 751-8987

**Golden Gate National Recreation
Area** ☎ 556-0560

Golden Gate Park Tennis
☎ 753-7101

Moscone Recreation Center
☎ 292-2006

Parks and Recreation Department
☎ 831-2700

Presidio National Park ☎ 561-4323

**San Francisco School of
Windsurfing** ☎ 753-3235

Skates on Haight ☎ 752-8375

Stow Lake Boat Rentals
☎ 752-0347

Tilden Regional Park
☎ 510/843-2137

TOURS

Walking Tours:

All About Chinatown!
☎ 415/982-8839

**Art Deco Society of California
Walking Tours** ☎ 415/982-DECO

Bay Ventures ☎ 510/234-4834

California Historical Society
☎ 415/357-1848

City Guides Neighborhood Walks
☎ 557-4266

Cruisin' The Castro ☎ 550-8110

Flower Power Haight-Ashbury Tours
☎ 863-1621

Friends of Recreation and Parks
☎ 415/263-0991

Glorious Food Culinary Walktours
☎ 415/441-5637

Javawalk ☎ 415/673-WALK

**Mission District Mural Tours/Precita
Eye Mural Center** ☎ 285-2287

One Dollah Statue Walks
☎ 510/834-3617

Pacific Heights Heritage Walks
☎ 415/441-3000

Victorian Home Walk
☎ 415/252-9485

Wok Wiz Chinatown Tours
☎ 981-8989

Air Tours:

San Francisco Helicopter Tours
☎ 415/635-4500

San Francisco Seaplane Tours
☎ 415/332-4843

Bus & Van Tours:

Gray Line ☎ 558-9400

Great Pacific Tour ☎ 626-4499

Cruise Tours:

Blue and Gold Fleet ☎ 773-1188

Hornblower Dining Yachts
☎ 415/394-8900

Red and White Fleet ☎ 447-0597

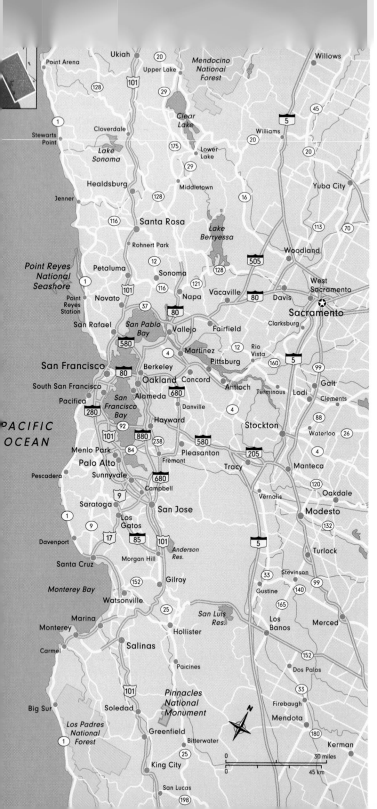

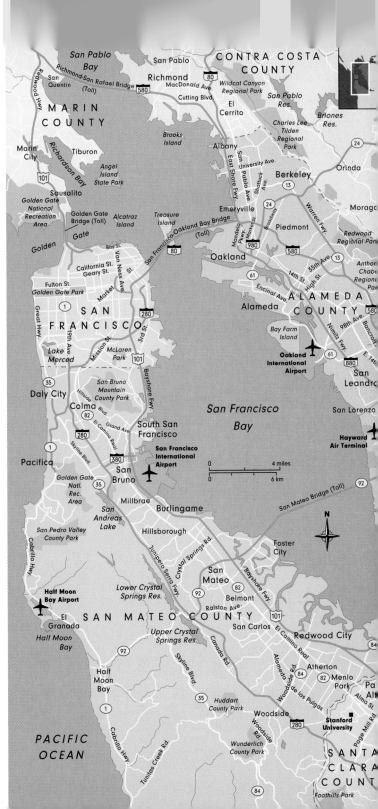

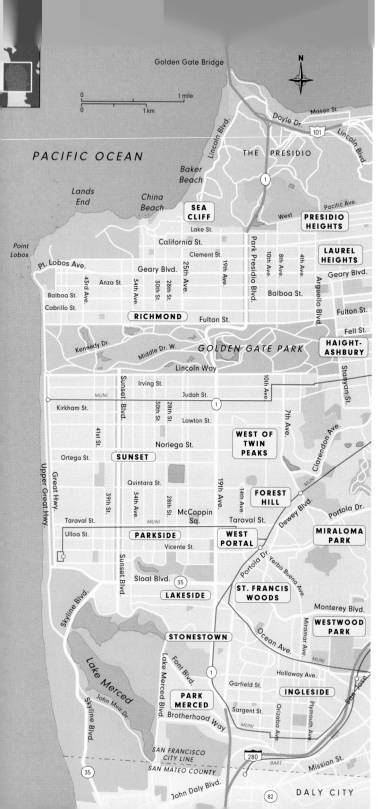

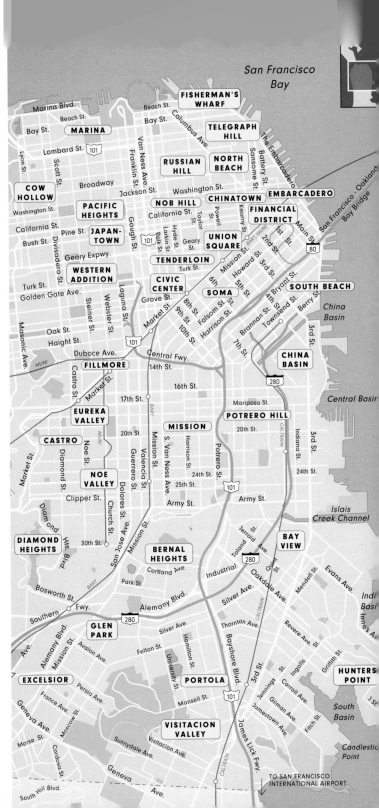

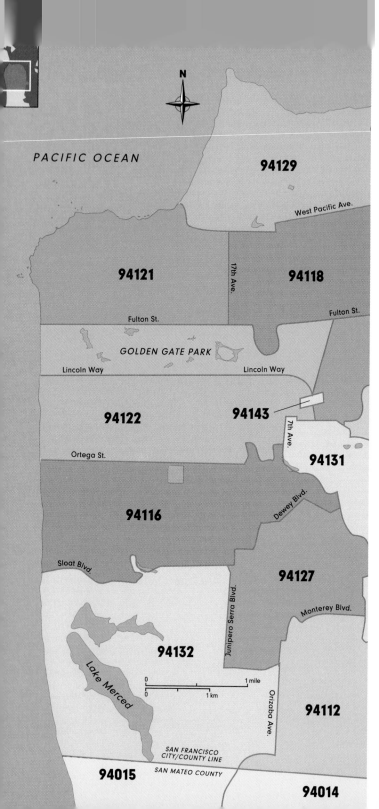

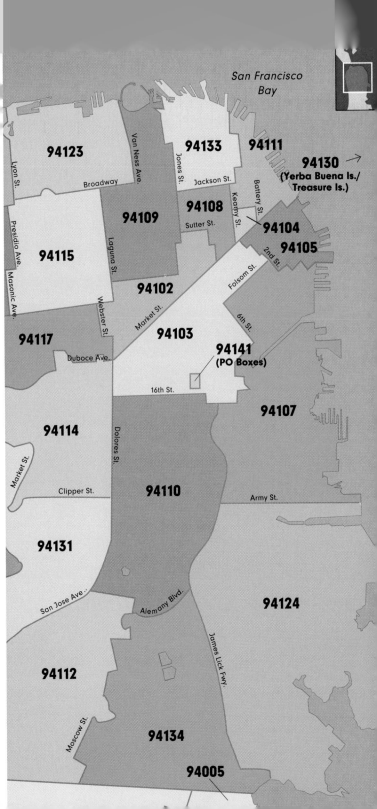

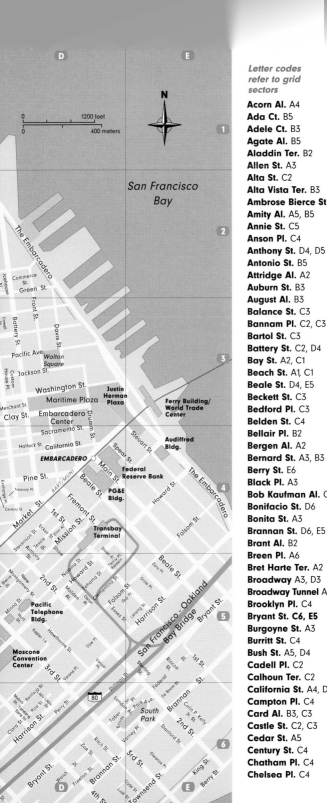

San Francisco
Bay

N

0   1200 feet
0   400 meters

The Embarcadero

Icehouse Al.
Commerce Al.
Green St.
Front St.
Battery St.
Davis St.
Pacific Ave.
Cowell Pl.
Custom House Pl.
Jackson St.
Walton Square

Washington St.
Maritime Plaza
Justin Herman Plaza
Clay St.
Merchant St.
Embarcadero Center
Drumm St.
Sacramento St.
Halleck St.
California St.
Ferry Building/ World Trade Center
Audiffred Bldg.

Steuart St.

EMBARCADERO

Pine St.
Exchange Pl.
Treasury Pl.
Century St.
Spear St.
Main St.
Beale St.
Fremont St.
Federal Reserve Bank
PG&E Bldg.
Howard St.
The Embarcadero

Market St.
1st St.
2nd St.
Ecker St.
Elim Al.
Stevenson St.
Jessie St.
Anthony St.
Shaw Al.
Mission St.
Minna St.
Howard St.
Natoma St.
Tehama St.
Clementina St.
Folsom St.
Oscar Al.
Guy Pl.
Lansing St.
Essex St.
Transbay Terminal
Shoen Al. Pl.
Tehama Al. Beldam
Zeno Pl.
Circle Pl.
Beale St.
Harrison St.
Bryant St.

A. Barse
New Montgomery St.
A. Barse Pl.
Pacific Telephone Bldg.
Minna St.
Maiden
Malden
Hawthorne St.
Kaplan La.
Doe Pl.
Vassar Pl.
San Francisco - Oakland Bay Bridge
Sterling St.
Rincon St.
Federal St.
De Boom St.
1st St.
Bryant St.

Moscone Convention Center
3rd St.
Verona Pl.
Sullivan St.
J St.
London St.
South Park
Taber Pl.
South
Park Ave.
Varney Pl.
Colin P. Kelly Jr. St.
Stanford St.
2nd St.

Mabini St.
Bonifacio St.
Lapu Lapu St.
Rizal St.
Tandang St.
Clara St.
Harrison St.
Perry St.
Ritch St.
Zoe St.
Brannan St.
80
3rd St.
Clarence Pl.

Bryant St.
Welsh St.
Freelon St.
4th St.
Townsend St.
Clyde St.
Lusk St.
King St.
Berry St.

Letter codes refer to grid sectors on preceding map

Chestnut St. A2, C2
Child St. C2
Churchill St. B3
Clara St. C6, D6
Clarence Pl. E6
Claude La. C4
Clay St. A4, D3
Clementina St. C6, D5
Clyde St. E6
Codman Pl. B3, B4
Cohen Pl. B5
Colin Pl. B5
C. P. Kelly Jr. St. E6
Columbus Ave. A1, C3
Commerce St. D2
Commercial St. C4, D4
Cooper Al. C3
Cordelia St. C3
Cosmo Pl. B5
Cowell Pl. D3
Culebra Ter. A2
Cushman St. B4
Custom House Pl. D3
Cyril Magnin St. B5, C5
Cyrus Pl. A3
Darrell Pl. C2
Dashiell Hammett St. C4
Davis St. D2, D4
Dawson Pl. B4
DeBoom St. E6
Delgado Pl. A3
Delta Pl. B4
Derby St. B5
Dodge St. A6
Doric Al. B3
Dow Pl. D5
Drumm St. D3, D4
Duncombe Al. C3
Dunne's Al. C3
Eastman St. A3
Eaton Pl. B3
Ecker St. D4
Eddy St. A5, C5
Edgardo Pl. C2
Edith St. C2
8th St. B6
Elim Al. D4
Ellis St. A5, C5
Elm St. A6
Elwood St. B5
Embarcadero, The B1, E4
Emery La. B3
Emma St. C4
Essex St. D5, E5
Ewer Pl. B4
Fallon Pl. B3
Falmouth St. C6

Federal St. E6, E5
Fella Pl. C4
Fern St. A5
Fielding St. B2
5th St. C5, D6
Filbert St. A3, C2
1st St. D4, E6
Fisher Al. B3
Florence St. B3
Folsom St. C6, E4
4th St. C5, D6
Francisco St. A2, C2
Frank St. B4
Frank Norris St. A4
Franklin St. A6
Freelon St. D6
Freeman Ct. B4
Fremont St. D4, E5
Fresno St. C3
Front St. D2, D4
Gallagher La. C6
Geary St. A5, C5
Genoa Pl. C2
Gerke Al. C2
Gibb St. C3
Glover St. A3, B3
Gold St. C3
Golden Ct. B4
Golden Gate Ave. A6, B6
Grant Ave. C1, C5
Green St. A3, D2
Greenwich St. A2, C2
Grote Pl. E5
Grove St. A6
Guy Pl. D5, E5
Halleck St. D4
Hangah St. C4
Hardie Pl. C4
Harlan Pl. C4
Harlem Al. B5
Harriet St. C6
Harrison St. C6, E4
Hastings Ter. A3
Havens St. A2
Hawthorne St. D5
Hayes St. A6
Helen St. A4
Hemlock St. A5
Himmelman Pl. B3
Hobart Al. B5
Hodges Al. C3
Holland Ct. C5
Hooker Al. B4
Hotaling Pl. C3
Houston St. B2
Howard St. B6, E4
Hulbert Al. C6
Hunt St. D5

Hyde St. A1, B6
Icehouse Al. D2
Ils La. C3
Isadora Duncan La. B5
Ivy St. A6
Jack Kerouac Al. C3
Jack London Al. D6, E6
Jackson St. A4, D3
James Al. C3
Jansen St. B2
Jason Ct. C3
Jasper Pl. C2, C3
Jefferson St. A1, B1
Jerome Al. C3
Jessie St. B6, D4
John St. B3
Jones St. A1, B6
Joice St. C4
Julia St. B6
Julius St. C2
Kaplan La. D5
Kearny St. C1, C5
Kenneth Roxroth Pl. C3
Kent St. B2
Keyes Al. B3
Kimball Pl. A4
King St. E6
Kramer Pl. C2
Krausgrill Pl. C2
La Ferrera Ter. C2
Lansing St. E5
Lapu Lapu St. D6
Larch St. A6
Larkin St. A1, A6
Leavenworth St. A1, B6
Lech Walesa St. A6
Leidesdorff St. C4, D4
Leroy Pl. B4
Lick Pl. C4
Lombard St. A2, C2
Lurmont Ter. A2
Lusk St. D6, E6
Lynch St. A3
Lysette St. B4
Mabini St. D6
Macondray La. A3, B3
Maiden La. C5
Main St. D4, E5
Malden Al. D5
Malvina Pl. B4
Marcy Pl. B3
Margrave Pl. C3
Marion Pl. B2, B3
Mark La. C4
Mark Twain Pl. D3
Market St. A6, D4
Mary St. C6
Mason St. B1, B5

Hercules

Pinole

El Sobrante

CONTRA COSTA COUNTY

San Pablo

San Rafael

San Pablo Bay

Richmond-San Rafael Bridge (Toll)

1 **2**

S.F. Drake Blvd.

Redwood Hwy.

San Quentin

Richmond

580

MacDonald Ave.
Cutting Blvd.

Wildcat Regional Park

San Pablo Res.

Briones Res.

El Cerrito

MARIN COUNTY

Brooks Island

Charles Lee Tilden Regional Park

Muir Woods National Monument

Richardson Bay

Tiburon

Albany

3
Berkeley

Shattuck Ave.

San Pablo Ave.

East Shore Fwy.

4
13

Angel Island State Park

Golden Gate National Recreation Area

Sausalito

101

Golden Gate

Alcatraz Island

Treasure Island

San Francisco-Oakland Bay Bridge (Toll)

24

5

Broadway

Piedmont

6

Warren Fwy.

24

Golden Gate Bridge (Toll)

19 **17** **15**

80

980

7

MacArthur Fwy.

Golden Gate

20 **18** **16**

Bay St.
B'way

14

Van Ness Ave.

13

3rd St.

8

580

35th Ave.

13

21
22
23

Geary Blvd.

Oakland

14th St.

High St.

61

Golden Gate Park

12

Market St.

280

11

ALAMEDA COUNTY

24

1

10

Encinal Ave.

Alameda

25

SAN FRANCISCO

19th Ave.

3rd St.

9

Bay Farm Island

880

Nimitz Fwy.

Lake Merced

Mission St.

McLaren Park

101

Bayshore Fwy.

San Francisco Bay

Oakland International Airport

61

N

Daly City

26

San Bruno State Park

Hillside Blvd.

35

82

El Camino Real

Grand Ave.

South San Francisco

1

280

380

San Francisco International Airport

0   8 miles

0   12 km

Pacifica

27

Skyline Blvd.

Golden Gate Natl. Rec. Area

San Bruno

Millbrae

Burlingame

San Mateo Bridge (Toll)

92

San Andreas Lake

35

Hillsborough

82

Foster City

San Pedro Valley County Park

Cabrillo Hwy.

Junipero Serra Fwy.

Crystal Springs Rd.

San Mateo

92

Bayshore Fwy.

Half Moon Bay Airport

Lower Crystal Springs Res.

Belmont

Ralston Ave.

28

El Granada

SAN MATEO COUNTY

Upper Crystal Springs Res.

San Carlos

El Camino Real

101

Redwood City

Half Moon Bay

Canada Rd.

29

Alameda de las Pulgas

84

Atherton

82

Menlo Park

PACIFIC OCEAN

KEY

1 Hospitals

11 24-Hour Pharmacies

92

35

Huddart County Park

Woodside

280

Stanford University

1

Listed by Site Number

1 Ross Hospital
2 Marin General
3 Alta Bates-Herrick Campus
4 Alta Bates Medical Center
5 Children's Hospital Oakland
6 Kaiser-Oakland Campus
7 Summit Medical Center
8 Alameda Co Med Ctr-Highland Campus
9 St. Luke's Hospital
10 San Francisco General Hospital
11 Walgreens
12 Davies Medical Center
13 St. Francis Memorial Hospital
14 Chinese Hospital
15 Calif Pacific Med Ctr-Pacific Campus
16 Pacific Coast Hospital
17 Walgreens
18 Mount Zion Medical Center
19 Kaiser-Geary Campus
20 California Pacific Med Ctr-East Campus
21 California Pacific Med Ctr-Calif Campus
22 St.Mary's Medical Center
23 Kaiser-French Campus
24 UCSF Medical Center
25 Laguna Honda Hospital
26 Walgreens
27 Walgreens
28 CPC Belmont Hills Hospital
29 Sequoia Hospital

Listed Alphabetically   Area Code (415) unless otherwise noted.

HOSPITALS

Alameda Co Medical Center–Highland Campus, 8. 1411 E 31st St, Oakland ☎ 510/437-4800

Alta Bates Medical Center, 4. 2450 Ashby Ave, Berkeley ☎ 510/204-4444

Alta Bates–Herrick Campus, 3. 2001 Dwight Way, Berkeley ☎ 510/845-0130

California Pacific Medical Center–California Campus, 21. 3700 California St ☎ 387-8700

California Pacific Medical Center–East Campus, 20. 3698 California St ☎ 387-8700

California Pacific Medical Center–Pacific Campus, 15. 2333 Buchanan St ☎ 563-4321

CPC Belmont Hills Hospital, 28. 1301 Ralston Ave, Belmont ☎ 593-2143

Children's Hospital, 5. 747 52nd St, Oakland ☎ 510/428-3000

Chinese Hospital, 14. 845 Jackson St ☎ 982-2400

Davies Medical Center, 12. Castro St & Duboce Ave ☎ 565-6000

Kaiser Permanente–French Campus, 23. 4131 Geary Blvd ☎ 202-2000

Kaiser Permanente–Geary Campus, 19. 2425 Geary Blvd ☎ 510/596-7600

Kaiser Permanente–Oakland Campus, 6. 280 W MacArthur Blvd, Oakland ☎ 510/596-7600

Laguna Honda Hospital, 25. 375 Laguna Honda Blvd ☎ 664-1580

Marin General Hospital, 2. 250 Bon Air Rd, Greenbrae ☎ 925-7000

Mount Zion Medical Center, 18. 1600 Divisadero St ☎ 567-6600

Pacific Coast Hospital, 16. 1210 Scott St ☎ 563-3444

Ross Hospital, 1. 1111 Sir Francis Drake Blvd, Kentfield ☎ 800/786-7677

St. Francis Memorial Hospital, 13. 900 Hyde St ☎ 353-6000

St. Luke's Hospital, 9. 3555 Cesar Chavez St ☎ 647-8600

St. Mary's Medical Center, 22. 450 Stanyan St ☎ 668-1000

San Francisco General Hospital, 10. 1001 Potrero Ave ☎ 206-8000

Sequoia Hospital, 29. 170 Alameda Ave, Redwood City ☎ 369-5811

Summit Medical Center, 7. 350 Hawthorne Ave, Oakland ☎ 510/869-6600

UCSF Medical Center, 24. 505 Parnassus Ave ☎ 476-1000

24-HOUR PHARMACIES

Walgreens, 11. 498 Castro St ☎ 861-6276

Walgreens, 17. 3201 Divisadero St ☎ 931-6417

Walgreens, 26. 395 S Mayfair Ave, Daly City ☎ 756-4535

Walgreens, 27. 2238 Westborough Blvd, South San Francisco ☎ 873-0551

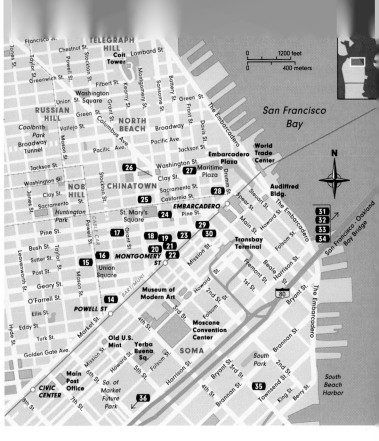

San Francisco Bay

TELEGRAPH HILL
NORTH BEACH
CHINATOWN
SOMA
CHINA BASIN
POTRERO
BAY VIEW
PORTOLA

Listed Alphabetically
PUBLIC

Area Code (415) unless otherwise noted.
PROFESSIONAL

Main Library, 18. Larkin, between Grove & Fulton Sts ☎ 557-4400

Anza, 26. 550 37th Ave ☎ 666-7160

Bayview/Anna E. Waden, 48. 5075 3rd St ☎ 715-4100

Bernal, 46. 500 Cortland Ave ☎ 695-5160

Blind & Print Handicapped Library, 17. 100 Larkin St ☎ 557-4253

Chinatown, 15. 1135 Powell St ☎ 274-0275

Eureka Valley/Harvey Milk Mem, 31. 3555 16th St ☎ 554-9445

Excelsior, 44. 4400 Mission St ☎ 337-4735

Glen Park, 45. 653 Chenery St ☎ 337-4740

Golden Gate Valley, 4. 1801 Green St ☎ 292-2195

Ingleside, 42. 387 Ashton Ave ☎ 337-4745

Marina, 3. 1890 Chestnut St ☎ 292-2150

Merced, 41. 155 Winston Dr ☎ 337-4780

Mission, 35. 3359 24th St ☎ 695-5090

Noe Valley/Sally Brunn, 36. 451 Jersey St ☎ 695-5095

North Beach, 5. 2000 Mason St ☎ 274-0270

Ocean View, 43. 111 Broad St ☎ 337-4785

Ortega, 37. 3223 Ortega St ☎ 753-7120

Park, 30. 1833 Page St ☎ 666-7155

Parkside, 38. 1200 Taraval St ☎ 753-7125

Portola, 47. 2450 San Bruno Ave ☎ 715-4090

Potrero, 34. 1616 20th St ☎ 695-6640

Presidio, 24. 3150 Sacramento St ☎ 292-2155

Richmond, 25. 351 9th Ave ☎ 666-7165

Sunset, 29. 1305 18th Ave ☎ 753-7130

Visitacion Valley, 49. 45 Leland Ave ☎ 337-4790

West Portal, 39. 190 Lenox Way ☎ 753-7135

Western Addition, 22. 1550 Scott St ☎ 292-2160

Alliance Francaise, 16. 1345 Bush St ☎ 775-7755

Annual Reports Library, 6. 369 Broadway ☎ 956-8665

California Academy of Sciences, 27. Music Concourse, Golden Gate Park ☎ 750-7102

California Genealogical Society, 8. 300 Brannan St ☎ 777-9936

California Historical Society, 10. 678 Mission St ☎ 357-1848

Federal Reserve Bank Library, 7. 101 Market St ☎ 974-3216

Gay and Lesbian Historical Society of Northern California, 9. 973 Market St ☎ 777-5455

Goethe Institut, 14. 530 Bush St ☎ 391-0428

Holocaust Center of Northern California, 32. 601 14th Ave ☎ 751-6040

Japanese American Nat'l Library, 21. 1619 Sutter St ☎ 567-5006

Libraria Cristiana, 33. 3126 16th St ☎ 431-9027

Mechanics Institute, 12. 57 Post St ☎ 956-2196

Mills Law Library, 13. 220 Montgomery St ☎ 781-2665

Nat'l Maritime Museum Library, 2. Fort Mason Bldg E ☎ 556-9870

San Francisco African American Historical and Cultural Society, 1. Fort Mason, Bldg C ☎ 441-0640

San Francisco County Law, 19. City Hall, 401 Van Ness Ave ☎ 554-6821

San Francisco Performing Arts Library & Museum, 20. 399 Grove St ☎ 255-4800

San Francisco Psychoanalytic Institute Library, 23. 2420 Sutter St ☎ 563-4477

Sierra Club/William E. Colby Memorial Library, 11. 85 2nd St ☎ 977-5506

Strybing Arboretum Russell Library of Horticulture, 28. Golden Gate Park ☎ 661-1316

Sutro, 40. 480 Winston Dr ☎ 731-4477

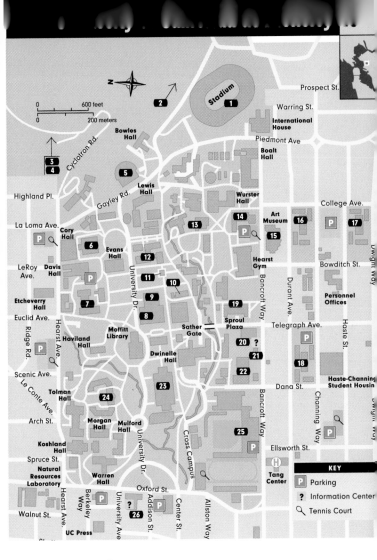

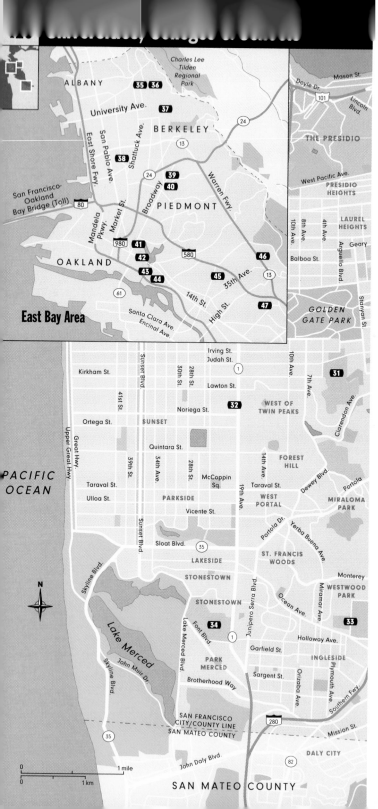

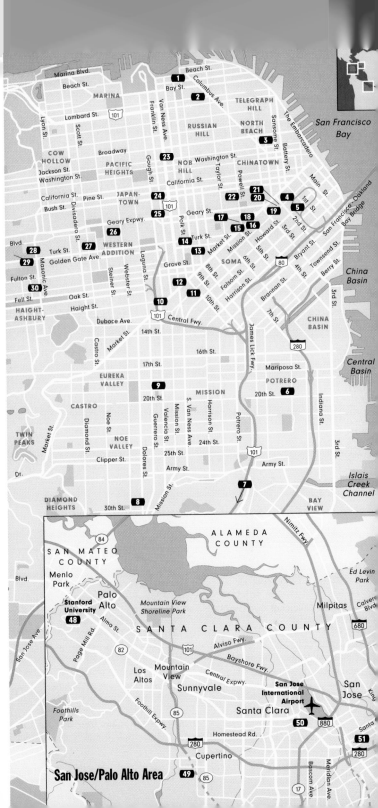

Listed by Site Number

MAP 11 San Francisco International Airport

101
Old Bayshore Hwy.
To Long-Term Parking
Bayshore Fwy.
TOP LEVEL:
Departures— national and international, lost and found, bank and bureau de change, duty-free shop, AT&T Communications Center, police & emergency services
MEZZANINE LEVEL:
Bank, nursery, police & emergency services, VIP conference room
LOWER LEVEL:
National and international arrivals, baggage claim, customs and immigration, bureau de change, car rental, hotel information
Car Rentals
Dollar
Budget
Avis
National
Hertz
Car Rentals
KEY
Parking
Bus and Shuttle Stops
SF Airport Hilton
Bayshore Fwy.
Old Bayshore Hwy.
To Alamo Car Rentals
Madrone St.
Bay St.
101

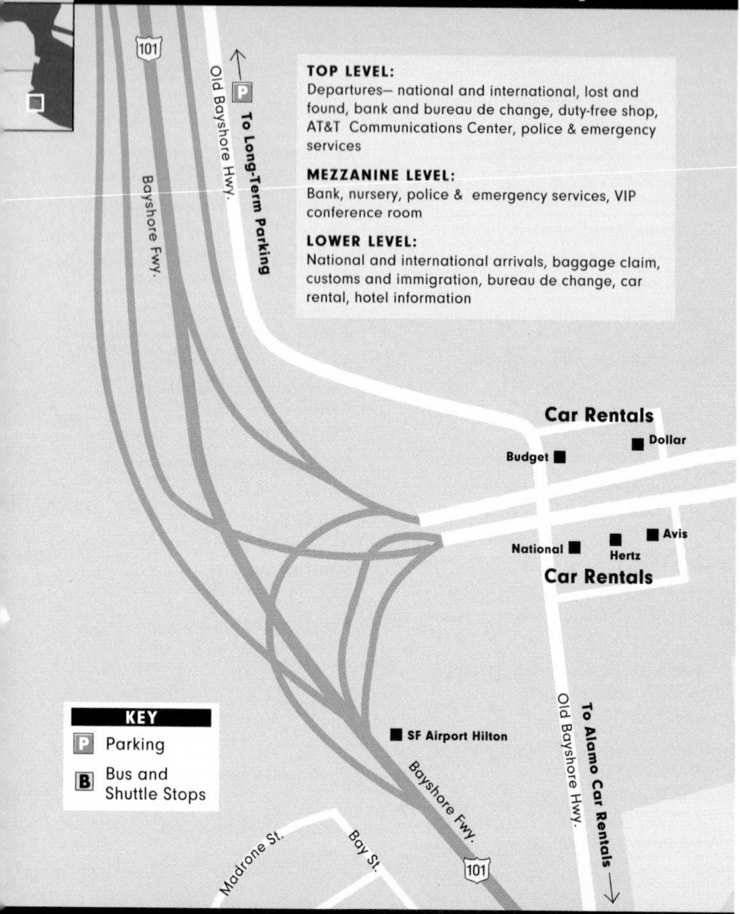

Airlines	Terminal A	B	C	D	E	F
Aeroflot ☎ 800/995-5555				●		
Air Canada ☎ 800/776-3000	●					
Air China ☎ 415/392-2156				●		
Air France ☎ 800/237-2747				●		
Alaska ☎ 800/426-0333				●		
Allegro ☎ 415/583-8891				●		
America West ☎ 800/235-9292		●				
American Airlines ☎ 800/433-7300					●	
American Eagle ☎ 800/433-7300					●	
American Trans Air ☎ 800/435-9282		●				
Asiana ☎ 800/227-4262				●		
British Airways ☎ 800/247-9297				●		
Canadian ☎ 800/426-7000					●	
China Airlines ☎ 800/227-5118				●		
Continental Airlines ☎ 800/525-0280		●				
Delta ☎ 800/221-1212			●			
EVA Air ☎ 800/695-1188				●		
Finnair ☎ 800/950-5000				●		
Frontier ☎ 800/432-1359		●				
Hawaiian Air ☎ 800/367-5320				●		
Japan Air Lines ☎ 800/525-3663				●		
Korean Air ☎ 415/956-6373				●		
KLM Airlines ☎ 800/374-7747				●		
LACSA ☎ 800/225-2272				●		

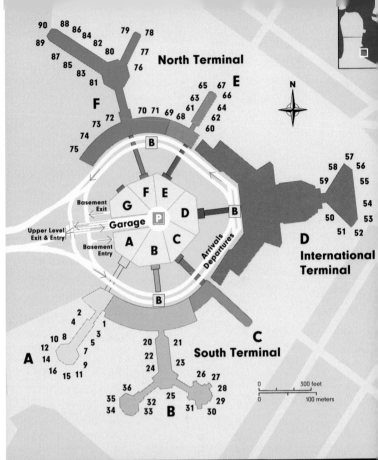

Airlines (cont.) Terminal	A	B	C	D	E	F
LTU International Airways				●		
Lufthansa ☎ 800/645-3880				●		
Mexicana ☎ 800/531-7921				●		
Midwest Express ☎ 800/452-2022		●				
Northwest (Domestic) ☎ 800/225-2525			●			
(International) ☎ 800/447-4747				●		
Philippine Air Lines ☎ 800/435-9725				●		
Reno Air ☎ 800/736-6247			●			
Rich International		●				
Shuttle by United ☎ 800/748-8853						●
Singapore Airlines ☎ 800/742-3333				●		
Skywest/Delta Connection ☎ 800/221-1212			●			
Southwest Airlines ☎ 800/435-9792	●					
TACA ☎ 800/535-8780				●		
Tower Air ☎ 800/221-2500				●		
TWA ☎ (Domestic) ☎ 800/221-2000		●				
(International) ☎ 800/892-4141		●				
United (Domestic) ☎ 800/241-6522						●
(International) ☎ 800/538-2929				●		
United Express ☎ 800/241-6522						●
USAir ☎ 800/428-4322	●					
USAir Express ☎ 800/428-4322	●					
Virgin Atlantic ☎ 800/862-8621				●		
Western Pacific ☎ 800/930-3030					●	

MAP 12

Oakland & San Jose Int'l Airports

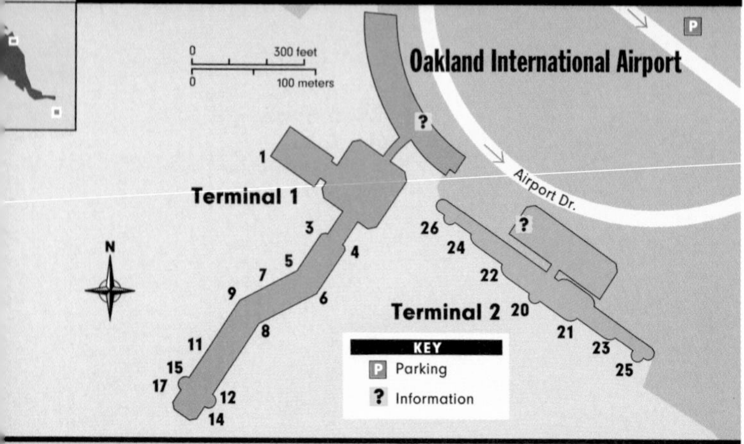

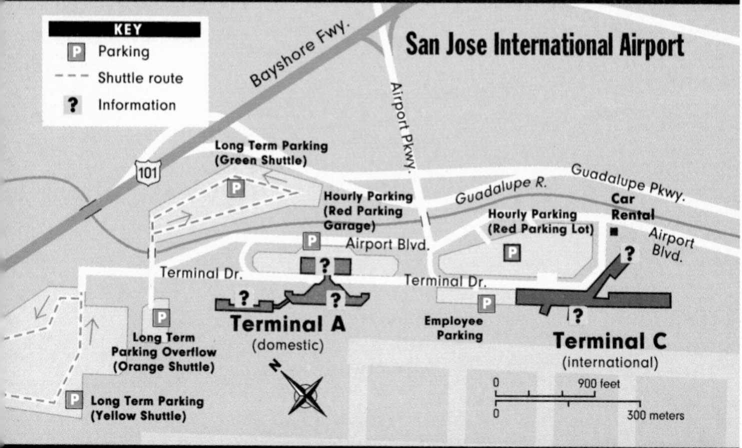

Oakland International Airport

0 ___ 300 feet	
0 ___ 100 meters	

Airport Dr.

Terminal 1

1
3
5   4
7
9   6
8
11
15
17
12
14

26
24
22   20
21   23
25

Terminal 2

N

KEY
P Parking
? Information

San Jose International Airport

KEY
P Parking
- - - Shuttle route
? Information

Bayshore Fwy.

Airport Pkwy.

Guadalupe R.

Guadalupe Pkwy.

Long Term Parking
(Green Shuttle)

Hourly Parking
(Red Parking
Garage)

Hourly Parking
(Red Parking Lot)

Car
Rental

Airport
Blvd.

Airport Blvd.

Terminal Dr.

Terminal Dr.

Terminal A
(domestic)

Employee
Parking

Terminal C
(international)

Long Term
Parking Overflow
(Orange Shuttle)

Long Term Parking
(Yellow Shuttle)

0 ___ 900 feet
0 ___ 300 meters

Oakland International   Terminal ① ②

	1	2
DOMESTIC		
Alaska Airlines ☎ 800/426-0333	●	
America West ☎ 800/235-9292	●	
American Airlines ☎ 800/443-7300	●	
Delta Air Lines ☎ 800/221-1212	●	
Horizon Air ☎ 800/547-9308	●	
Southwest Airlines ☎ 800/435-9792	●	●
United Airlines/Shuttle by United ☎ 800/241-6522	●	
INTERNATIONAL		
Martinair Holland ☎ 800/627-8462	●	
Taesa Airlines ☎ 800/328-2372	●	

San Jose International   Terminal Ⓐ Ⓒ

	A	C
American Airlines ☎ 800/443-7300	●	
Reno Air/Reno Air Express ☎ 800/736-6247	●	
Southwest Airlines ☎ 800/435-9792	●	
Alaska Airlines/Horizon Air ☎ 800/426-0333		●
America West Airlines ☎ 800/235-0280		●
Continental ☎ 800/525-0280		●
Delta Air Lines ☎ 800/221-1212		●
Mexicana Airlines ☎ 800/531-7921		●
Northwest/KLM Airlines ☎ 800/225-2525		●
Skywest/The Delta Connection ☎ 800/221-1212		●
TWA ☎ 800/221-2000		●
United/United Express ☎ 800/241-6522		●

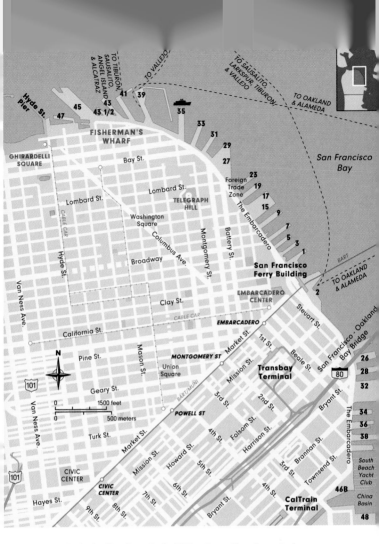

Listed Alphabetically   Area Code (415) unless otherwise noted.

BUS AND TRAIN SERVICE

MUNI ☎ 673-6864

BART ☎ 992-2278 or 510/465-2278

CalTrain 4th and Townsend Sts
☎ 800/660-4287

Amtrak (Oakland and Emeryville)
☎ 800/872-7245

Cable Cars (MUNI) ☎ 673-6864

BUS TERMINALS

Transbay Terminal,
1st and Mission Sts

FERRY SERVICE

Alameda-Oakland Ferry, from
Alameda and Jack London Sq. in
Oakland to Pier 39 & Ferry Bldg in SF
☎ 510/522-3300

Blue & Gold Fleet, from Pier 41 and
SF Ferry Bldg to Tiburon, Sausalito,
Angel Island, Alcatraz ☎ 773-1188

Golden Gate Ferry, from SF Ferry
Bldg to Sausalito and Larkspur
☎ 923-2000

Harbor Bay Ferry, from Harbor Bay
Isle near Oakland Airport to SF Ferry
Bldg, Pier 41 and 3Com Park
☎ 510/769-5500

Vallejo Baylink Ferry, from SF Ferry
Bldg and Pier 39 to Angel Island and
Vallejo ☎ 707/643-3779

CRUISE SHIP PASSENGER TERMINAL
Pier 35 ☎ 765-5300

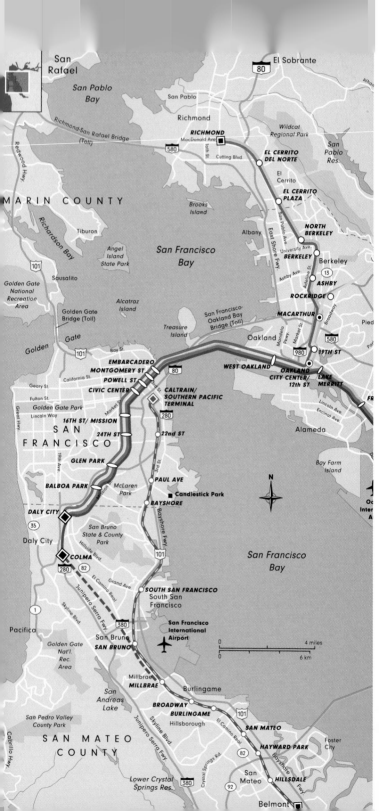

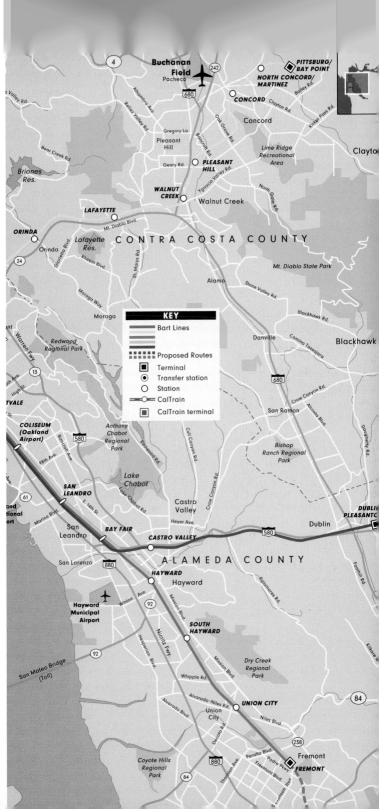

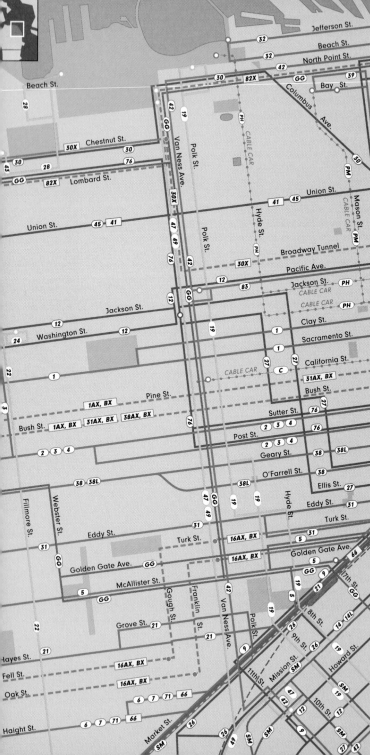

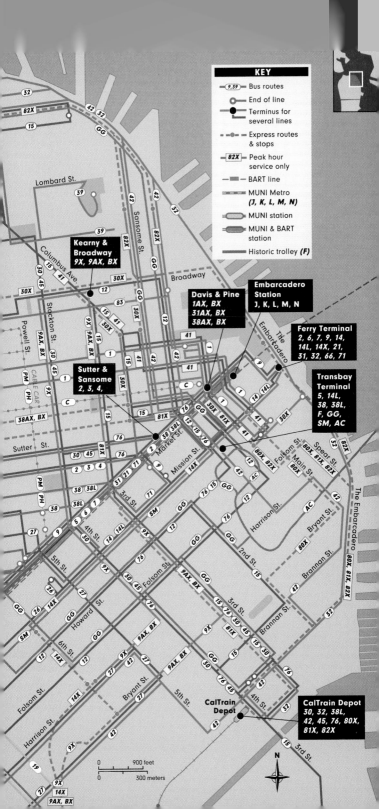

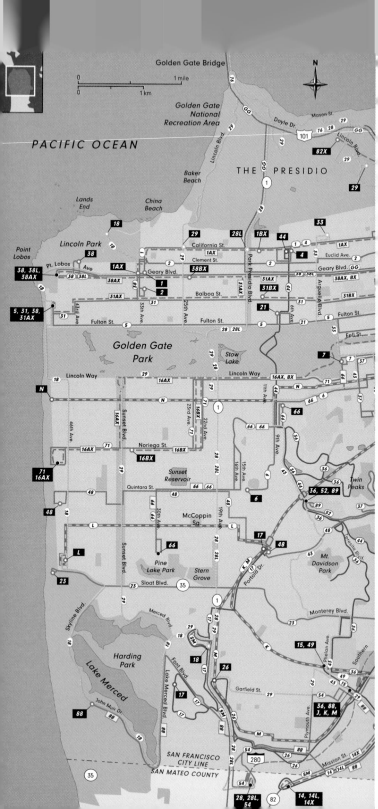

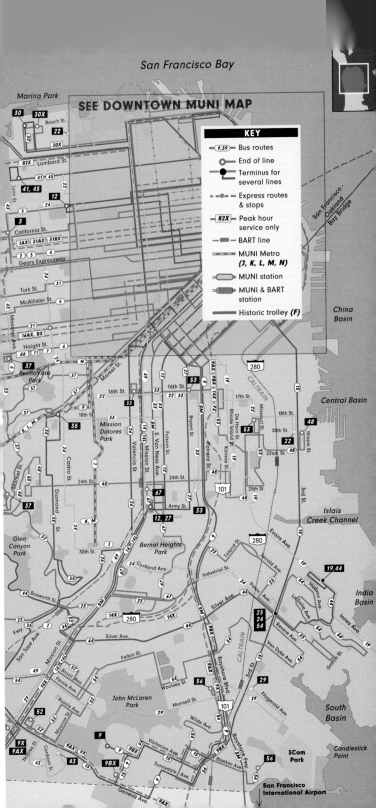

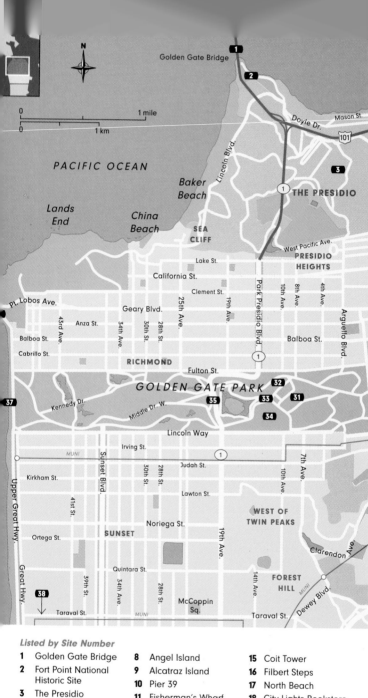

San Francisco Bay

Marina Blvd.

MARINA

Beach St.

Lombard St.

Lincoln Blvd.

Lyon St.

Scott St.

COW HOLLOW

Broadway

Washington St.

California St.

LAUREL HEIGHTS

Bush St.

Geary Blvd.

Divisadero St.

Masonic Ave.

Golden Gate Ave.

Fulton St.

Fell St.

HAIGHT-ASHBURY

Oak St.

Haight St.

Duboce Ave.

Steiner St.

Webster St.

Laguna St.

Gough St.

Castro St.

Market St.

14th St.

17th St.

EUREKA VALLEY

CASTRO

20th St.

Noe St.

Diamond St.

22nd St.

NOE VALLEY

Church St.

Clipper St.

TWIN PEAKS

Market St.

Van Ness Ave.

Franklin St.

PACIFIC HEIGHTS

Jackson St.

JAPAN-TOWN

Pine St.

Geary Expwy.

WESTERN ADDITION

Turk St.

Beach St.

Bay St.

Columbus Ave.

TELEGRAPH HILL

RUSSIAN HILL

NORTH BEACH

CHINATOWN

Washington St.

NOB HILL

California St.

Hyde St.

Taylor St.

Larkin St.

Polk St.

Turk St.

Grove St.

8th St.

9th St.

10th St.

Harrison St.

Market St.

Powell St.

Kearny St.

Geary St.

SOMA

Mission St.

Howard St.

Folsom St.

Bryant St.

Brannan St.

Townsend

4th St.

5th St.

6th St.

7th St.

3rd St.

2nd

1st

The Embarcadero

Battery St.

Sansome St.

BART/MUNI

Central Fwy.

16th St.

MISSION

Valencia St.

Guerrero St.

Dolores St.

Mission St.

S. Van Ness Ave.

Harrison St.

24th St.

25th St.

Army St.

James Lick Fwy.

Potrero St.

POTRERO

Mariposa St.

20th St.

Army St.

CALTRAIN

MUNI

BART

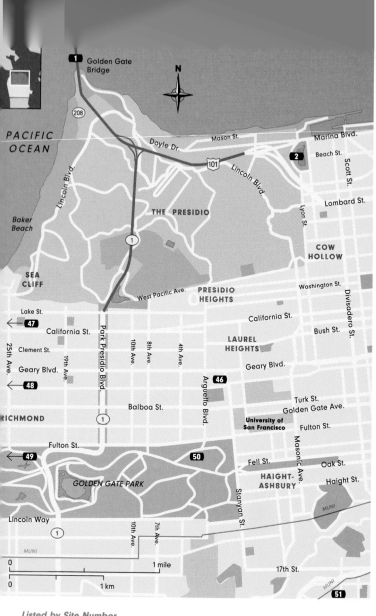

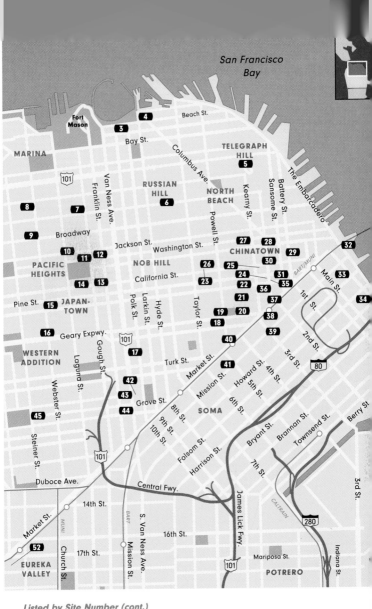

San Francisco Bay

Beach St.

Fort Mason

3

4

Bay St.

MARINA

TELEGRAPH HILL

5

Columbus Ave.

101

Van Ness Ave.

Franklin St.

RUSSIAN HILL

6

NORTH BEACH

Kearny St.

Battery St.

Sansome St.

The Embarcadero

8

7

Broadway

9

Jackson St.

Washington St.

CHINATOWN

27 28

29

32

10

11 12

NOB HILL

26

25

30

BART/MUNI

Main St.

33

PACIFIC HEIGHTS

California St.

24

31

Powell St.

1st St.

34

14 13

23

22 36 35

Pine St.

15

JAPAN-TOWN

Larkin St.

Hyde St.

Polk St.

Taylor St.

21

37

2nd St.

16

Geary Expwy.

19 20

38

Gough St.

101

18

39

3rd St.

WESTERN ADDITION

17

40

Laguna St.

Turk St.

Market St.

41

80

Webster St.

42

Mission St.

Howard St.

4th St.

5th St.

43

Grove St.

8th St.

SOMA

6th St.

Brannan St.

Townsend St.

Berry St.

44

Steiner St.

45

9th St.

Folsom St.

Bryant St.

7th St.

3rd St.

10th St.

Harrison St.

101

Duboce Ave.

Central Fwy.

James Lick Fwy.

CALTRAIN

280

14th St.

MUNI

BART

S. Van Ness Ave.

Market St.

Church St.

52

16th St.

Mission St.

Mariposa St.

Indiana St.

EUREKA VALLEY

17th St.

POTRERO

Listed by Site Number (cont.)

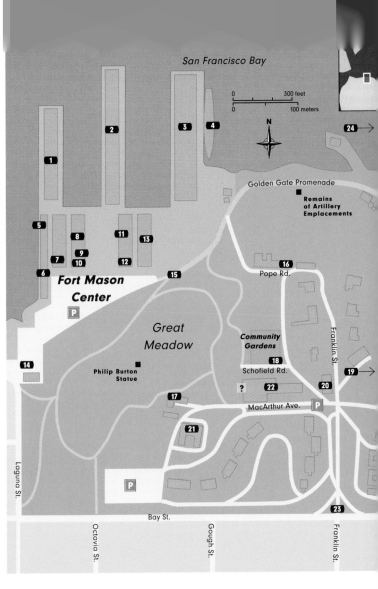

San Francisco Bay

300 feet
100 meters

N

Golden Gate Promenade

**Remains
of Artillery
Emplacements**

Pope Rd.

**Fort Mason
Center**

P

*Great
Meadow*

**Philip Burton
Statue**

*Community
Gardens*

Schofield Rd.

?

MacArthur Ave.

P

Laguna St.

Octavia St.

Gough St.

Franklin St.

Franklin St.

Bay St.

P

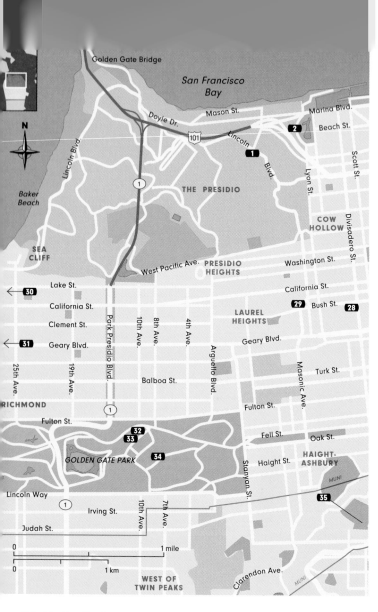

African-American Historical and Cultural Society, 4.
Fort Mason, Building C
☎ 441-0640

Ansel Adams Center for Photography, 26. 250 4th St
☎ 495-7000

Asian Art Museum, 33.
Golden Gate Park ☎ 379-8801

Cable Car Museum, 15.
1201 Mason St ☎ 474-1887

California Academy of Sciences, 34. Music Concourse Dr,
Golden Gate Park ☎ 750-7145
Laserium ☎ 750-7138
Morrison Planetarium ☎ 750-7141
Natural History Museum ☎ 750-7145
Steinhart Aquarium ☎ 750-7145

California Historical Society Museum, 22.
678 Mission St ☎ 357-1848

California Palace of the Legion of Honor, 30. Lincoln Park ☎ 750-3600

Cartoon Art Museum, 25.
814 Mission St ☎ 227-8666

Center for the Arts/Yerba Buena Gardens, 24.
701 Mission St ☎ 978-2787

Chinese Historical Society of America, 16.
650 Commercial St ☎ 391-1188

Exploratorium, 2. 3601 Lyon St
☎ 561-0360

Haas-Lilienthal House, 14. 2007
Franklin St ☎ 441-3004

Hyde Street Pier, 7.
Foot of Hyde St ☎ 556-3002

Jewish Museum San Francisco, 19.
121 Steuart St ☎ 543-8880

MH de Young Memorial Museum, 32.
Golden Gate Park ☎ 863-3330

Mexican Museum, 6.
Fort Mason, Building D ☎ 441-0404

Musée Mécanique, 31.
1090 Point Lobos ☎ 386-1170

Museo Italo-Americano, 5.
Fort Mason, Building C ☎ 673-2200

Museum of the City of San Francisco, 11. 2801 Leavenworth St
☎ 928-0289

Museum of Russian Culture, 28.
2450 Sutter St ☎ 921-4082

National Maritime Museum, 12.
900 Beach St ☎ 556-3002

Octagon House, 13.
2645 Gough St ☎ 441-7512

Pacific Heritage Museum, 17.
608 Commercial St ☎ 399-1124

Presidio Museum, 1.
Lincoln Blvd & Funston Ave
☎ 561-4331

Randall Museum, 35.
199 Museum Way ☎ 554-9600

Ripley's Believe It Or Not Museum, 10. 175 Jefferson St
☎ 771-6188

San Francisco Craft and Folk Art Museum, 3. Fort Mason, Building A
☎ 775-0990

San Francisco Fire Department Museum, 29. 655 Presidio Ave
☎ 558-3546

San Francisco Museum of Modern Art, 23.
151 3rd St ☎ 357-4000

San Francisco Performing Arts Library and Museum, 27.
399 Grove St ☎ 255-4800

SS *Jeremiah O'Brien*, 20.
Pier 32, foot of Brannan St
☎ 441-3101

Treasure Island Museum, 21.
Treasure Island ☎ 395-5067

USS *Pampanito* World War II Submarine, 8.
Pier 45, Fisherman's Wharf
☎ 929-0202

Wax Museum Entertainment Complex, 9. 145 Jefferson St
☎ 800/439-4305

Wells Fargo Museum, 18. 420
Montgomery St ☎ 396-2619

M.H. de Young & Asian Art Museum

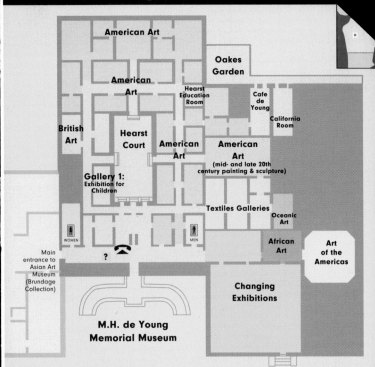

American Art

American Art

Oakes Garden

Hearst Education Room

Cafe de Young

California Room

British Art

Hearst Court

American Art

American Art
(mid- and late 20th century painting & sculpture)

Gallery 1: Exhibition for Children

WOMEN

MEN

Textiles Galleries

Oceanic Art

Main entrance to Asian Art Museum (Brundage Collection)

?

African Art

Art of the Americas

Changing Exhibitions

M.H. de Young Memorial Museum

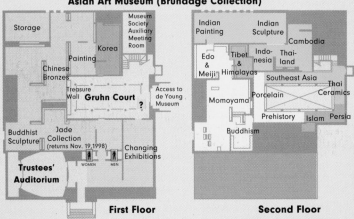

Asian Art Museum (Brundage Collection)

Storage

Museum Society Auxiliary Meeting Room

Korea

Painting

Chinese Bronzes

Treasure Wall

Gruhn Court

?

Access to de Young Museum

Buddhist Sculpture

Jade Collection (returns Nov. 19, 1998)

WOMEN   MEN

Changing Exhibitions

Trustees' Auditorium

First Floor

Indian Painting

Indian Sculpture

Cambodia

Edo & Meiji

Tibet & Himalayas

Indonesia

Thailand

Momoyama

Southeast Asia

Porcelain

Thai Ceramics

Prehistory

Islam

Persia

Buddhism

Second Floor

ASIAN ART MUSEUM: KEY TO GALLERIES (BY COUNTRY OR REGION)

China

Islamic & Ancient Persian Art

India

Southeast Asia

Japan

Tibet & Himalayas

Korea

MAP
22

Harbor

Gashouse
Cove

Marina Blvd.

1

**Mexican
Museum**

Fort
Mason

*Golden Gate
Recreation
Area*

Bay St.

*Aquatic
Park*

Jefferson St.

Beach St.

**Maritime
Museum**

Jones St.

Taylor St.

Ghirardelli
Square

North Point St.

Bay St.

*Russian
Hill Park*

2

3

George R.
Moscone
Recreation
Center

Francisco St.

101

Greenwich St.

Chestnut St.

Lombard St.

Hyde St.

Greenwich St.

Polk St.

Larkin St.

Filbert St.

Leavenworth St.

Jones St.

**UNION
STREET**

Laguna St.

Octavia St.

Gough St.

Franklin St.

Van Ness Ave.

Green St.

Vallejo St.

Broadway
Tunnel

Fillmore St.

Webster St.

Buchanan St.

Broadway

Pacific Ave.

Jackson St.

Washington St.

Webster St.
Historic
District

Clay St.

Lafayette
Plaza

Larkin St.

Hyde St.

Jones St.

CABLE CAR

**Pacific
Med. Ctr.**

Sacramento St.

CABLE CAR

FILLMORE

California St.

Octavia St.

Franklin St.

101

Pine St.

Bush St.

Webster St.

Bush St.

Gough St.

Van Ness Ave.

Sutter St.

Post St.

14

Geary St.

Steiner St.

**Japanese Cultural
& Trade Center**

Laguna St.

**St. Mary's
Cathedral**

Polk St.

Larkin St.

Hyde St.

Leavenworth St.

Hamilton
Square

St. Francis
Square

Ellis St.

Fillmore St.

Webster St.

Eddy St.

Ellis St.

Jefferson
Square

Gough St.

Elm St.

Golden Gate Ave.

Steiner St.

**WESTERN
ADDITION**

Turk St.

McAllister St.

31

**City
Hall**

Civic
Center

**CIVIC
CENTER**

Alamo Sq.
Historic
District

Golden Gate Ave.

McAllister St.

Fulton St.

Octavia St.

Grove St.

9th St.

Alamo
Square

Grove St.

Ivy St.

32

Franklin St.

Hayes St.

Van Ness Ave.

10th St.

33 34

Hayes St.

Linden St.

Pierce St.

Fell St.

Oak St.

101

Page St.

VAN NESS
Ⓜ

MUNI

BART

Mission St.

Howard St.

35

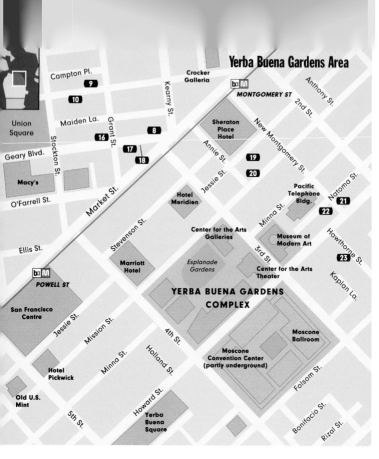

Yerba Buena Gardens Area

Listed Alphabetically   Area Code (415) unless otherwise noted.

Academy of Art College Fine Art Gallery, 13. 625 and 688 Sutter St ☎ 274-2234

Academy of Art College Sculpture Center, 5. 410 Bush St ☎ 274-8683

American Indian Contemporary Arts, 16. 23 Grant Ave ☎ 989-7003

Art Exchange, 17. 77 Geary St ☎ 956-5750

Artists Forum, 10. 251 Post St ☎ 981-6347

Aurobora Press, 22. 147 Natoma St ☎ 546-7880

Banaker Gallery, 10. 251 Post St ☎ 397-1397

Bomani Gallery, 10. 251 Post St ☎ 296-8677

Braunstein-Quay Gallery, 7. 250 Sutter St ☎ 392-5532

Bucheon Gallery, 34. 355 Hayes St ☎ 863-2891

Catharine Clark Gallery, 18. 49 Geary St ☎ 399-1439

Campbell-Theibaud Gallery, 3. 645 Chestnut St ☎ 441-8680

Capp Street Project, 24. 525 2nd St ☎ 495-7101

Crown Point Press, 23. 20 Hawthorne St ☎ 974-6273

Dorothy Weiss Gallery, 6. 256 Sutter St ☎ 397-3611

Ebert Gallery, 18. 49 Geary St ☎ 296-8405

Edith Caldwell Gallery, 10. 251 Post St ☎ 989-5414

Eleonore Austerer Gallery, 12. 540 Sutter St ☎ 986-2244

Four Walls, 35. 3160-A 16th St ☎ 626-8515

Fraenkel Gallery, 18. 49 Geary St ☎ 543-5155

Galería de la Raza 27. 2857 24th St ☎ 826-8009

Gallery Paule Anglim, 8. 14 Geary St ☎ 433-2710

George Krevsky Fine Art, 17. 77 Geary St ☎ 397-9748

Hackett Freedman Gallery, 7. 250 Sutter St ☎ 362-7152

Haines Gallery, 18. 49 Geary St ☎ 397-8114

Joanne Chappell Gallery, 25. 625 2nd St ☎ 777-5711

Meridian Gallery, 11. 545 Sutter St ☎ 398-7229

Meyerovich Gallery, 10. 251 Post St ☎ 421-7171

Michael Dunev Gallery, 19. 660 Mission St ☎ 284-9851

Michael Shapiro Gallery, 7. 250 Sutter St ☎ 398-6655

Mulligan-Shanoski Gallery, 14. 747 Post St ☎ 771-0663

New Langton Arts, 29. 1246 Folsom St ☎ 626-5416

Olga Dollar Gallery, 9. 210 Post St ☎ 398-2297

Polanco Gallery of Mexican Arts, 33. 393 Hayes St ☎ 252-5753

Rena Bransten Gallery, 17. 77 Geary St ☎ 982-3292

Robert Koch Gallery, 18. 49 Geary St ☎ 421-0122

SF Camerawork, 21. 115 Natoma St ☎ 764-1001

San Francisco Art Commission Gallery, 31. 401 Van Ness Ave ☎ 554-6080

San Francisco Art Institute Walter McBean Gallery, 2. 800 Chestnut St ☎ 749-4545

San Francisco Museum of Modern Art Rental Gallery, 1. Fort Mason, Bldg A ☎ 441-4777

SOMAR Gallery, 26. 934 Brannan St ☎ 552-2131

Southern Exposure, 28. 401 Alabama St ☎ 863-2141

Stephen Wirtz Gallery, 18. 49 Geary St ☎ 433-6879

Terrain, 20. 165 Jessie St ☎ 543-0656

The Victoria Room, 30. 180 6th St ☎ 255-0364

Vorpal Gallery, 32. 393 Grove St ☎ 397-9200

Washington Square Gallery, 4. 1821 Powell St ☎ 291-9255

Weinstein Gallery, 15. 383 Geary St ☎ 362-8151

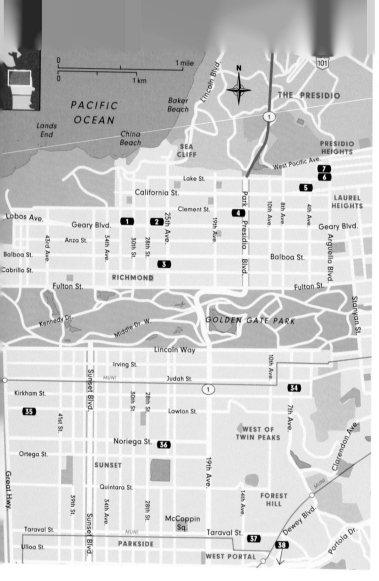

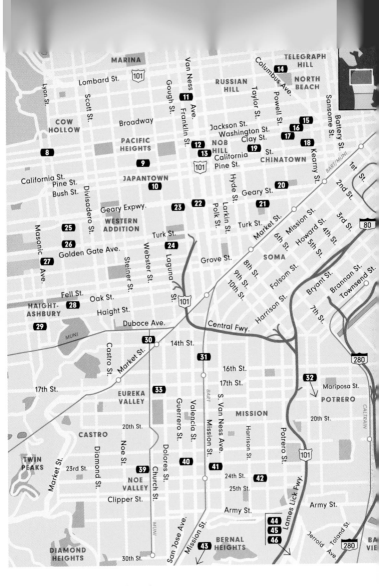

Adath Israel, 36.
1851 Noriega St ☎ 564-5665.
Jewish/Orthodox

All Saints' Church, 29. 1350 Waller St
☎ 621-1862. Episcopal

Allen Chapel, 44.
195 Scotia Ave ☎ 468-8406. African
Methodist Episcopal

Apostolic Faith Church, 45.
100 Felton St ☎ 468-1652

Assyrian Church of the East, 35.
3939 Lawton St ☎ 753-1869. Apostolic

Beth Sholom, 4. 1301 Clement St
☎ 221-8736. Jewish/Conservative

Bethel AME, 24.
970 Laguna St ☎ 921-4935

Buddha's Universal Church, 15.
720 Washington St ☎ 982-6116

Calvary Apostolic Church, 46.
1869 Oakdale Ave ☎ 642-1234

Chevra Thilim, 3. 751 25th Ave
☎ 752-2866. Jewish

Christ United Presbyterian Church, 10.
1700 Sutter St ☎ 567-3988

**Dignity San Francisco Gay,
Lesbian, Bisexual, and
Transgender Catholics, 34.**
1329 7th Ave ☎ 681-2491

**First African Methodist Episcopal
Zion Church, 27.**
2159 Golden Gate Ave ☎ 931-7479

**First Congregational Church of San
Francisco, 20.**
432 Mason St ☎ 392-7461

**Glide Memorial United Methodist
Church, 21.** 330 Ellis St ☎ 771-6300

**Good Samaritan Episcopal
Church, 43.** 459 Vienna St
☎ 586-8864

Grace Cathedral, 19. 1051 Taylor St
☎ 749-6310. Episcopal

**Holy Trinity Orthodox Cathedral,
11.** 1520 Green St ☎ 673-8565.

Holy Virgin Cathedral, 2.
6210 Geary Blvd ☎ 221-3255.
Russian Orthodox

Kong Chow Temple, 17.
855 Stockton St ☎ 434-2513. Buddhist

**Lincoln Park Presbyterian
Church, 1.** 417 31st Ave ☎ 751-1140

Mission Dolores, 33. 3321 16th St
☎ 621-8203. Catholic

Mission Presbyterian Church, 41.
23rd & Capp Sts ☎ 647-8295

Mt Zion Baptist Church, 28.
1321 Oak St ☎ 863-4109

Noe Valley Ministry, 39. 1021
Sanchez St ☎ 282-2317. Presbyterian

Old First Presbyterian Church, 13.
1751 Sacramento St ☎ 776-5552

Old St Mary's Cathedral, 18. 660
California St ☎ 288-3840. Catholic

Portalhurst Presbyterian Church, 37.
321 Taraval St ☎ 664-5335

St Cyprian's Episcopal Church, 26.
2097 Turk St ☎ 567-1855

St Francis Lutheran Church ELCA, 30.
152 Church St ☎ 621-2635

**St Gregory Nyssen Episcopal
Church, 32.**
500 De Haro St ☎ 255-1552

St James Catholic Church, 40.
1086 Guerrero St ☎ 824-4232

St James' Episcopal Church, 5.
4620 California St ☎ 751-1198

**St John the Baptist Serbian
Orthodox Church, 25.**
910 Baker St ☎ 567-5869

**St John the Evangelist Episcopal
Church, 31.** 1661 15th St ☎ 861-1436

St John's Presbyterian Church, 7.
Arguello Blvd & Lake St ☎ 751-1626

St Luke's Episcopal Church, 12.
Van Ness Ave & Clay St ☎ 673-7327

St Mark's Lutheran Church, 22.
1111 O'Farrell St ☎ 928-7770

St Mary's Cathedral, 23.
1111 Gough St ☎ 567-2020. Catholic

St Peter's Catholic Church, 42.
1200 Florida St ☎ 282-1652

Sts Peter and Paul Church, 14.
666 Filbert St ☎ 421-0809. Catholic

Sherith Israel, 9. 2266 California St
☎ 346-1720. Jewish

Swedenborgian Church, 8.
2107 Lyon St ☎ 346-6466

Tin Hou Temple, 16.
125 Waverly Pl ☎ 391-4841. Buddhist

Temple Emanu-El, 6. Arguello Blvd &
Lake St ☎ 751-2535. Jewish

**Wright Chapel African Methodist
Episcopal Church, 38.**
627 Capitol Ave ☎ 239-9727

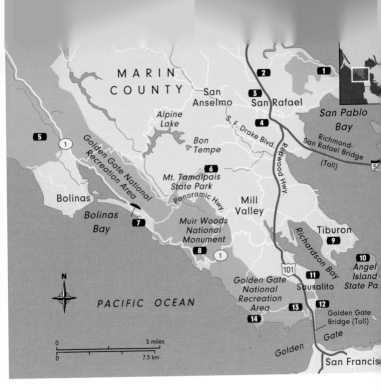

MAP 28 Exploring/The Southern Peninsula

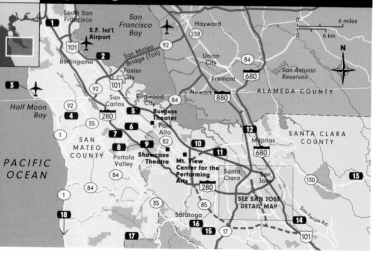

Listed by Site Number

1 Acres of Orchids
2 Coyote Point Mus for Environmental Ed
3 Fitzgerald Marine Reserve
4 Obester Winery
5 Barbie Hall of Fame
6 Stanford Museum of Art/Rodin Sculpture Garden
7 Filoli State Historic Landmark
8 Stanford Linear Accelerator
9 Stanford University
10 NASA Ames Research Center
11 Paramount's Great America
12 Garbage Museum
13 J Lick Observatory
14 Mirassou Vineyards
15 Villa Montalvo Center for the Arts
16 Hakone Japanese Garden
17 Big Basin Redwoods State Park
18 Año Nuevo State Reserve

Listed Alphabetically   Area Code (650) unless otherwise noted.

Acres of Orchids, 1. 1450 El Camino Real, South San Francisco ☎ 871-5655

Año Nuevo State Reserve, 18. Hwy 1, Pescadero ☎ 879-0227

Barbie Hall of Fame, 5. 433 Waverly St, Palo Alto ☎ 326-5841

Big Basin Redwoods State Park, 17. Hwy 236, Boulder Creek ☎ 408/338-8860

Coyote Point Museum for Environmental Education, 2. 1651 Coyote Point Dr, San Mateo ☎ 342-7755

Filoli State Hist Landmark, 7. Cañada Rd, Woodside ☎ 364-2880

Garbage Museum, 12. 1601 Dixon Landing Rd, Milpitas ☎ 408/262-1401

Hakone Japanese Garden, 16. 21000 Big Basin Way, Saratoga ☎ 408/741-4994

James Lick Observatory, 13. Mt Hamilton Rd, San Jose ☎ 408/274-5061

James V Fitzgerald Marine Reserve, 3. Hwy 1, Moss Beach ☎ 728-3584

Mirassou Vineyards, 14. 3000 Aborn Rd, San Jose ☎ 408/274-4000

NASA Ames Research Center, 10. Moffet Field, Mountain View ☎ 604-5000

Obester Winery, 4. 12341 San Mateo Rd, Half Moon Bay ☎ 726-9463

Paramount's Great America, 11. 1 Great America Parkway, Santa Clara ☎ 408/988-1776

Stanford Linear Accelerator, 8. 2575 Sand Hill Rd, Menlo Park ☎ 926-2204

Stanford Museum of Art/Rodin Sculpture Garden, 6. Museum Way & Lomita Dr, Palo Alto ☎ 723-2560

Stanford University, 9. University Ave, Palo Alto ☎ 723-2300

Villa Montalvo Center for the Arts, 15. 15400 Montalvo Rd, Saratoga ☎ 408/961-5800

Listed by Site Number

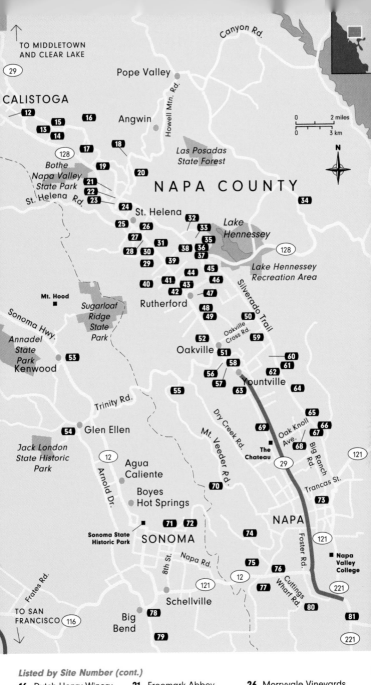

Flora Springs Winery, 29. 1978 W Zinfandel La, St Helena ☎ 963-5711

Franciscan Oakville Estates, 39. 1178 Galleron Rd, Rutherford ☎ 963-7111

Freemark Abbey Winery, 21. 3022 St Helena Hwy, St Helena ☎ 963-9694

Girard Winery, 50. 7717 Silverado Trail, Oakville ☎ 944-8577

Gloria Ferrer Champagne Caves, 78. 23555 Hwy 121, Sonoma ☎ 996-7256

Goosecross Cellars, 59. 1119 State La, Yountville ☎ 944-1986

Graeser Winery, 11. 255 Petrified Forest Rd, Calistoga ☎ 942-4437

Grgich Hills Cellar, 42. 1829 St Helena Hwy, Rutherford ☎ 963-2784

Hakusan Sake Gardens, 81. 1 Executive Way, Napa ☎ 258-6160

Heitz Wine Cellars, 31. 500 Taplin Rd, St Helena ☎ 963-3542

The Hess Collection, 70. 4411 Redwood Rd, Napa ☎ 255-1144

Hop Kiln Winery, 7. 6050 Westside Rd, Healdsburg ☎ 433-6491

Joseph Phelps Vineyards, 33. 200 Taplin Rd, St Helena ☎ 963-2745

Kendall-Jackson California Coast Wine Center, 8. 5007 Fulton Rd, Fulton ☎ 571-7500

Kenwood Vineyards, 53. 9592 Sonoma Hwy, Kenwood ☎ 833-5891

Korbel Winery, 5. 13250 River Rd, Guerneville ☎ 887-2294

Kornell Champagne Cellars, 17. 1091 Larkmead La, Calistoga ☎ 942-0859

Louis M. Martini, 27. 254 S St Helena Hwy, St Helena ☎ 963-2736

Lytton Springs Winery, 2. 650 Lytton Springs Rd, Healdsburg ☎ 433-7721

Markham Winery, 23 2812 N St Helena Hwy, St Helena ☎ 963-5292

Merryvale Vineyards, 26. 1000 Main St, St Helena ☎ 963-7777

Milat Vineyards, 40. 1091 S St Helena Hwy, St Helena ☎ 963-0758

Mont St John Cellars, 76. 5400 Old Sonoma Rd, Napa ☎ 255-8864

Monticello Vineyards, 68. 4242 Big Ranch Rd, Napa ☎ 253-2802

Mumm Napa Valley, 45. 8445 Silverado Trail, Rutherford ☎ 942-3434

Newlan Vineyards, 69. 5225 Solano Ave, Napa ☎ 257-2399

Nichelini Vineyards, 36. 2950 Sage Canyon Rd, St Helena ☎ 963-0717

Peju Province Winery, 48. 8466 St Helena Hwy, Rutherford ☎ 963-3600

Pine Ridge Winery, 62. 5901 Silverado Trail, Napa ☎ 253-7500

Piper Sonoma, 4. 11447 Old Redwood Hwy, Healdsburg ☎ 433-8843

Plam Vineyards, 58. 6200 Washington St, Yountville ☎ 944-1102

Prager Winery & Port Works, 30. 1281 Lewelling La, St Helena ☎ 963-PORT

Quail Ridge Winery, 44. 1155 Mee La, St Helena ☎ 963-9783

Raymond Vineyard & Cellar, 38. 849 Zinfandel La, St Helena ☎ 963-3141

Robert Mondavi Winery, 52. 7801 St Helena Hwy, Oakville ☎ 259-9463

Robert Pecota Winery, 10. 3299 Bennett La, Calistoga ☎ 942-6625

Robert Pepi Winery, 51. 7585 St Helena Hwy, Oakville ☎ 944-2807

Rombauer Vineyards, 19. 3522 Silverado Trail, St Helena ☎ 963-5170

Round Hill Cellars, 22. 1680 Silverado Trail, St Helena ☎ 963-5251

Rustridge, 34. 2910 Lower Chiles Valley Rd, St Helena ☎ 965-2871

Rutherford Hill Winery, 35. 200 Rutherford Rd, Rutherford ☎ 963-7194

S. Anderson Winery, 60. 1473 Yountville Crossrd, Yountville ☎ 944-8642

Sequoia Grove Vineyards, 49. 8338 St Helena Hwy, Napa ☎ 944-2945

Stag's Leap Wine Cellars, 61. 5766 Silverado Trail, Napa ☎ 944-2020

Sterling Vineyards, 14. 1111 Dunaweal La, Calistoga ☎ 942-3300

Sebastiani Vineyards, 71. 389 4th St E, Sonoma ☎ 938-5532

Viansa Winery, 79. 25200 Arnold Dr, Sonoma ☎ 935-4700

Vincent Arroyo Winery, 12. 2361 Greenwood Ave, Calistoga ☎ 942-6995

V. Sattui Winery, 32. 1111 White La, St Helena ☎ 963-7774

William Hill Winery, 73. 1761 Atlas Peak Rd, Napa ☎ 224-4477

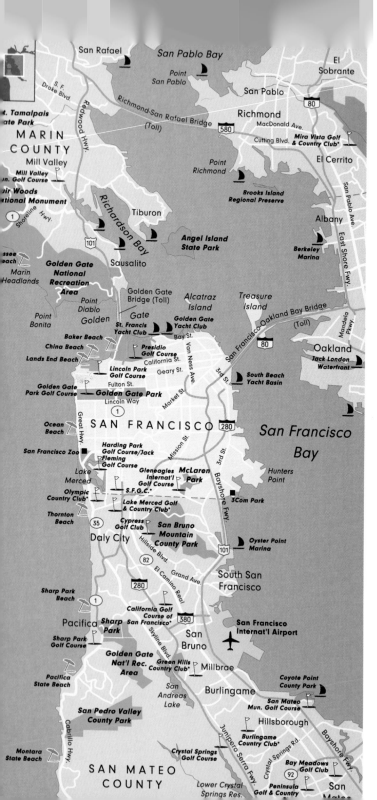

CONTRA COSTA COUNTY

Pacheco
Buchanan Fields
Golf & Country Club

242

Pleasant Hill
Golf & Country Club*

Pleasant Hill

680

Oak Grove Rd.

Bancroft Rd.

Heather Farms
Golf Club

Ygnacio Valley Rd.

Boundary Oaks
Golf Course

Walnut Creek

Wildcat Canyon
Regional
Park

San Pablo
Res.

Briones
Regional Park

Charles Lee
Tilden
Regional
Park

Briones
Res.

Tilden Park
Golf Club

University
Ave.

24

Lafayette Res.

Orinda

Round Hill Golf
and Country Club*

Berkeley

Shattuck Ave.

13

Rossmoor
Golf Club*

Alamo

Moraga

Claremont
Country Club*

24

B'way

Market St.

980

Piedmont

Warren Fwy.

Moraga
Country Club*

Les Trampas
Regional
Wilderness

Danville

Montclair
Golf Club

Redwood
Regional Park

680

580

13

35th Ave.

High St.

Upper San Leandro
Reservoir

San
Ramon

61

Barnhill
Marina

14th St.

ALAMEDA
COUNTY

Sequoyah
Country
Club*

Anthony
Chabot
Regional
Park

Cull Canyon Rd.

Redwood Rd.

Bishap Ranch
Regional Open
Space

Alameda

880

Encinal Ave.

Aeolian
Yacht Club

Bancroft Ave.

580

Lake Chabot
Mun. Golf
Course

Lake
Chabot

R.W. Crown
Mem. State
Beach

Willow Park
Golf Club

Alameda Mun.
Golf Course

61

Nimitz Fwy.

98th Ave.

Castro
Valley

580

Bay Farm
Island

Galbraith Mun.
Golf Course

E. 14th St.

Palomares Rd.

Oakland
Internat'l
Airport

Marina Golf Course

San
Leandro

San Leandro Marina

Tony Lema
Golf Course

238

San Lorenzo

Skywest
Golf Course

Hayward

Hayward
Regional
Shoreline

Hayward
Air Terminal

92

238

Hesperian Blvd.

Hayward
Regional
Shoreline

Hayward
Golf Course

Dry Creek
Pioneer
Regional Park

Mission Blvd.

880

92

San Mateo Bridge (Toll)

Whipple Rd.

N

Foster
City

0   4 miles
0   6 km

KEY

Beaches

Marinas

Golf Courses

*An asterisk with label
indicates private status

Coyote Hills
Regional
Park

84

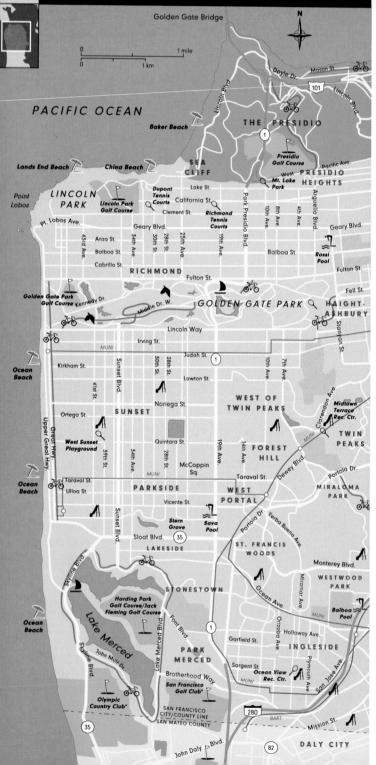

Golden Gate Bridge

N

0   1 mile
0   1 km

PACIFIC OCEAN

Doyle Dr.

Mason St.

101

Lincoln Blvd

Lincoln Blvd

THE PRESIDIO

Baker Beach

1

Presidio
Golf Course

Pacific Ave.

West
Mt. Lake
Park

PRESIDIO
HEIGHTS

Lands End Beach   China Beach

SEA
CLIFF

Lake St.

Park Presidio Blvd.

Arguello Blvd.

Point
Lobos

LINCOLN
PARK

Dupont
Tennis
Courts

Lincoln Park
Golf Course

California St.

Clement St.

Richmond
Tennis
Courts

10th Ave.

8th Ave.

4th Ave.

Geary Blvd.

Pt. Lobos Ave.

Geary Blvd.

25th St.

19th Ave.

Balboa St.

Rossi
Pool

43rd Ave.

Anza St.

34th Ave.

30th St.

28th St.

Fulton St.

Balboa St.

Cabrillo St.

RICHMOND

Fulton St.

Fell St.

Golden Gate Park
Golf Course

Kennedy Dr.

Middle Dr. W.

GOLDEN GATE PARK

HAIGHT-
ASHBURY

Stanyan St.

Lincoln Way

MUNI

Irving St.

Judah St.

1

10th Ave.

7th Ave.

Ocean
Beach

Kirkham St.

41st St.

Sunset Blvd.

30th St.

28th St.

Lawton St.

West of
Twin Peaks

Clarendon Ave.

Midtown
Terrace
Rec. Ctr.

Noriega St.

SUNSET

14th Ave.

MUNI

Twin
Peaks

Ortega St.

39th St.

34th Ave.

28th St.

Quintara St.

Forest
Hill

Dewey Blvd.

West Sunset
Playground

McCoppin
Sq.

19th Ave.

Taraval St.

Portola Dr.

Miraloma
Park

Ocean
Beach

Taraval St.

Ulloa St.

PARKSIDE

WEST
PORTAL

Yerba Buena Ave.

Sunset Blvd.

Vicente St.

Portola Dr.

Stern
Grove

Sava
Pool

St. Francis
Woods

Monterey Blvd.

Westwood
Park

Sloat Blvd.

35

LAKESIDE

Ocean Ave.

Miramar Ave.

Balboa
Pool

Skyline Blvd.

STONESTOWN

Ocean
Beach

Harding Park
Golf Course/Jack
Fleming Golf Course

Lake Merced

Lake Merced Blvd.

Font Blvd.

1

Oriziba Ave.

INGLESIDE

Garfield St.

Holloway Ave.

Plymouth Ave.

San Jose Ave.

Skyline Blvd.

John Muir Dr.

PARK
MERCED

MUNI

Sargent St.

Ocean View
Rec. Ctr.

Olympic
Country Club*

Brotherhood Way

San Francisco
Golf Club*

280

BART

Mission St.

SAN FRANCISCO
CITY/COUNTY LINE
SAN MATEO COUNTY

35

82

John Daly Blvd.

DALY CITY

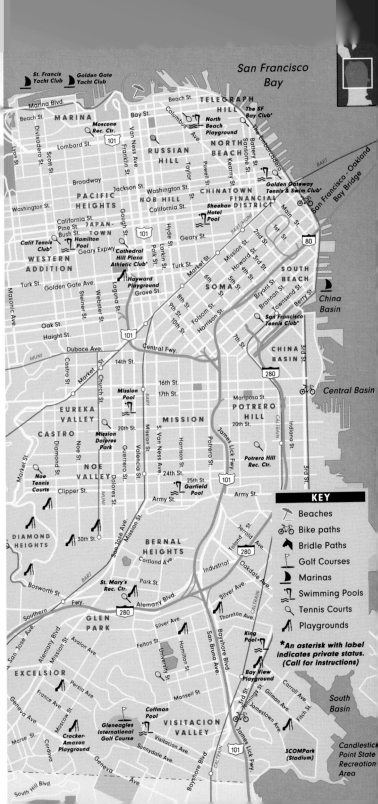

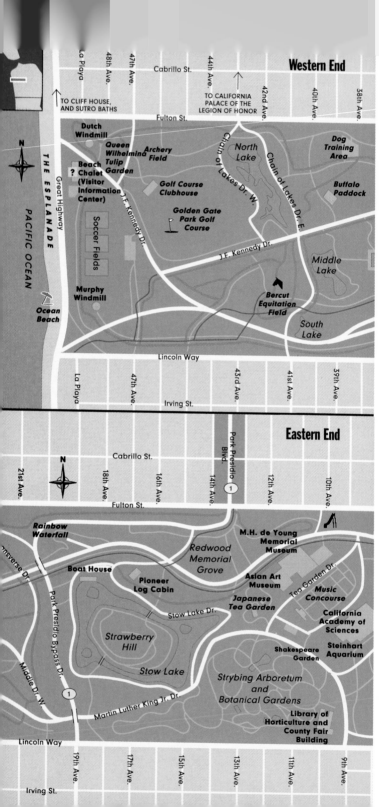

Western End

La Playa · 48th Ave. · 47th Ave. · Cabrillo St. · 44th Ave. · 42nd Ave. · 40th Ave. · 38th Ave.

TO CLIFF HOUSE, AND SUTRO BATHS

TO CALIFORNIA PALACE OF THE LEGION OF HONOR

Fulton St.

THE ESPLANADE

N

PACIFIC OCEAN

Dutch Windmill

Queen Wilhelmina Tulip Garden

Archery Field

North Lake

Dog Training Area

Beach Chalet (Visitor Information Center)

Chain of Lakes Dr. W.

Chain of Lakes Dr. E.

Buffalo Paddock

Golf Course Clubhouse

Soccer Fields

J.F. Kennedy Dr.

Golden Gate Park Golf Course

J.F. Kennedy Dr.

Middle Lake

Murphy Windmill

Bercut Equitation Field

South Lake

Ocean Beach

Lincoln Way

La Playa · 47th Ave. · 43rd Ave. · 41st Ave. · 39th Ave.

Irving St.

Eastern End

21st Ave. · 18th Ave. · 16th Ave. · Cabrillo St. · Park Presidio Blvd. · 14th Ave. · 12th Ave. · 10th Ave.

N

(1)

Fulton St.

Rainbow Waterfall

Transverse Dr.

M.H. de Young Memorial Museum

Redwood Memorial Grove

Boat House

Pioneer Log Cabin

Asian Art Museum

Tea Garden Dr.

Music Concourse

Park Presidio Bypass Dr.

Japanese Tea Garden

California Academy of Sciences

Stow Lake Dr.

Strawberry Hill

Shakespeare Garden

Steinhart Aquarium

Middle Dr. W.

Stow Lake

Strybing Arboretum and Botanical Gardens

(1)

Martin Luther King Jr. Dr.

Library of Horticulture and County Fair Building

Lincoln Way

19th Ave. · 17th Ave. · 15th Ave. · 13th Ave. · 11th Ave. · 9th Ave.

Irving St.

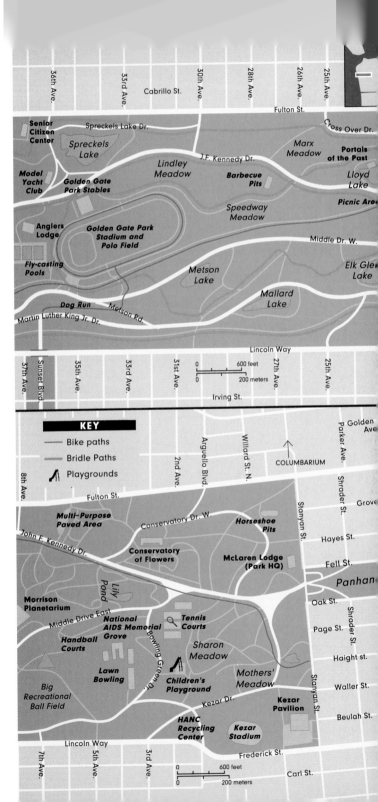

36th Ave.
33rd Ave.
Cabrillo St.
30th Ave.
28th Ave.
26th Ave.
25th Ave.
Fulton St.

Senior Citizen Center
Spreckels Lake Dr.
Spreckels Lake
Cross Over Dr.
Marx Meadow
Portals of the Past

Model Yacht Club
Golden Gate Park Stables
Lindley Meadow
J.F. Kennedy Dr.
Barbecue Pits
Lloyd Lake

Anglers Lodge
Golden Gate Park Stadium and Polo Field
Speedway Meadow
Picnic Area
Middle Dr. W.

Fly-casting Pools
Metson Lake
Elk Glen Lake

Dog Run
Metson Rd.
Mallard Lake

Martin Luther King Jr. Dr.

Lincoln Way

37th Ave.
Sunset Blvd.
35th Ave.
33rd Ave.
31st Ave.
27th Ave.
25th Ave.

0   600 feet
0   200 meters

Irving St.

KEY
— Bike paths
— Bridle Paths
🛝 Playgrounds

Golden Gate Ave
Parker Ave.

Arguello Blvd.
Willard St. N.
2nd Ave.
8th Ave.
↑ COLUMBARIUM

Fulton St.
Shrader St.
Grove

Multi-Purpose Paved Area
Conservatory Dr. W.
Horseshoe Pits
Hayes St.

John F. Kennedy Dr.
Conservatory of Flowers
McLaren Lodge (Park HQ)
Stanyan St.
Fell St.

Morrison Planetarium
Lily Pond
Oak St.
Panhan

Middle Drive East
National AIDS Memorial Grove
Page St.
Shrader St.

Handball Courts
Tennis Courts
Sharon Meadow
Haight st.

Lawn Bowling
Bowling Green Dr.
Children's Playground
Mothers' Meadow
Stanyan St.
Waller St.

Big Recreational Ball Field
Kezar Dr.
Kezar Pavilion
Beulah St.

HANC Recycling Center
Kezar Stadium

7th Ave.
5th Ave.
3rd Ave.
Lincoln Way
Frederick St.
Carl St.

0   600 feet
0   200 meters

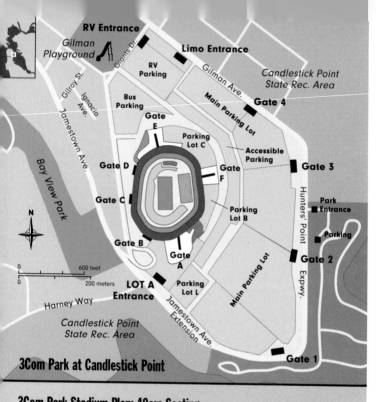

RV Entrance

Gilman Playground

Limo Entrance

Grants Dr.

RV Parking

Gilman Ave.

Candlestick Point State Rec. Area

Gate 4

Gilroy St.

Ignacio Ave.

Jamestown Ave.

Bus Parking

Main Parking Lot

Gate E

Parking Lot C

Accessible Parking

Gate 3

Gate D

Gate F

Bay View Park

Gate C

Parking Lot B

Park Entrance

Parking

Hunters' Point Expwy.

N

Gate B

Gate A

0 — 600 feet
0 — 200 meters

LOT A Entrance

Parking Lot L

Gate 2

Harney Way

Main Parking Lot

Candlestick Point State Rec. Area

Jamestown Ave. Extension

Gate 1

3Com Park at Candlestick Point

3Com Park Stadium Plan: 49ers Seating

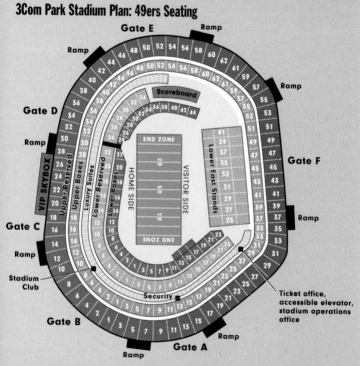

Gate E

Ramp

Ramp

48 50 52 54 56 58 60 62 61 59 57

44 46 48 50 52 54 56 58 60 62 61 59

Scoreboard

Gate D

Ramp

55 53 51

57 55 53

49 47 45

Gate F

END ZONE

Lower East Stands

41 39 37 35 33 31 29 27 25

VIP SKYBOX

Upper Reserved

Upper Boxes

Luxury Suites

Lower Reserved

Lower Boxes

HOME SIDE

VISITOR SIDE

Ramp

Gate C

Ramp

END ZONE

Stadium Club

Security

Ticket office, accessible elevator, stadium operations office

Gate B

Ramp

Gate A

Ramp

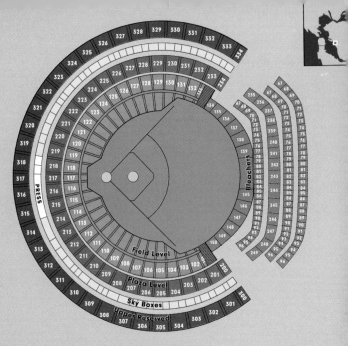

Oakland-Alameda County Coliseum Complex/Stadium

Oakland-Alameda County Coliseum Complex/Arena

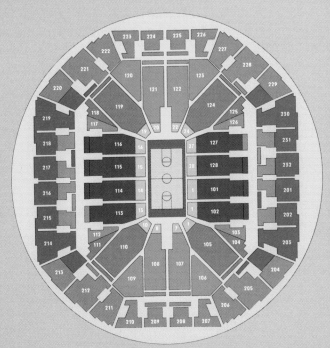

Grass Valley
Emigrant Gap
20
Tahoe National Forest
89
Hobart Mills
70
Wheatland
49
Colfax
80
Baxter
Truckee
Kings Beach
Lincoln
65
Tahoe City
28
431
39
Woodland
French Meadow Res.
Roseville
Auburn
80
Folsom Lake State Rec. Area
Hell Hole Res.
West Sacramento
5
80
Citrus Heights
Folsom
Lotus
Lake Tahoe
28
50
Sacramento
Placerville
Union Valley Res.
Camp Richardson
N E V A D A
Clarksburg
Placerville
Eldorado National Forest
S. Lake Tahoe
16
Kyburz
50
99
Plymouth
Kit Carson
Picketts Jct.
5
49
88
Woodfords
395
Galt
Ione
Jackson
88
Bear Valley
89
Lockeford
Camanche Res.
Pardee Res.
Pioneer
Topaz
Lodi
12
26
Camp Connell
4
Walker
88
Waterloo
26
New Hogan Res.
San Andreas
Dardanelle
Stanislaus National Forest
Toiyabe National Forest
Stockton
Angels Camp
4
Farmington
Copperopolis
Melones
Sonora
Pinecrest
Emigrant Wilderness
182
Manteca
120
New Melones Lake
108
Long Barn
Cherry Lake
Bridgeport Res.
Oakdale
Modesto
132
Waterford
Don Pedro Res.
Groveland
Lake Eleanor
Hetch Hetchy Res.
395
Bridgepo
49
Turlock
Turlock Lake
132
Lake McClure
Coulterville
Yosemite National Park
Lee Vining
99
Livingston
140
El Portal
Yosemite Village
Tuolumne Meadows
Mono Lake
Catheys Valley
140
Wawona
Inyo National Forest
Merced
Mariposa
Planada
152
Chowchilla
49
Lake Crowley
Dos Palos
Coarsegold
Oakhurst
Mammoth Pool Res.
Mammoth Lakes
33
41
395
Firebaugh
Madera
145
Millerton Lake
Lakeshore
168
Sierra National Forest
Florence Lake
Mendota
180
99
Tollhouse
Courtright Res.
168
B
Kerman
145
Clovis
168
Fresno
Pine Flat Res.
Wishon Res.
Big
Helm
Easton
Centerville
41
145
Five Points
Selma
Reedley
Squaw Valley
Kings Canyon National Park
269
Kingsburg
43
Orange Cove
180
180
198
Lemoore
Hanford
201
Orosi
Pinehurst
41
Visalia
Woodlake
245
Tulare Lake
43
63
198
Three Rivers
Sequoia National Park
Independence
Mt. Whitney (Highest Point in the Contiguous U.S.)
3
Kettleman City
Corcoran
Tulare
137
Exeter
Mineral King
Inyo National Forest
Lon
Pin
5
99
63
Lindsay
65
137
Sequoia National Forest

0   20 miles
0   30 km

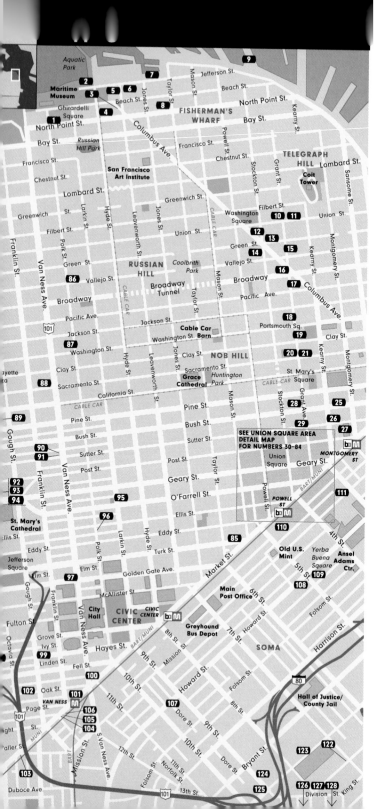

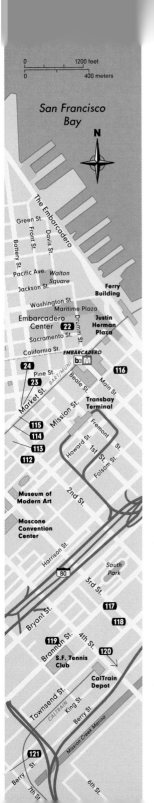

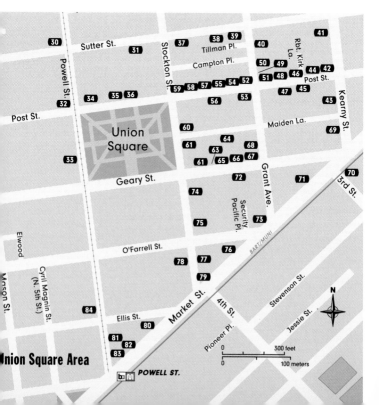

Union Square Area

DOWNTOWN

Abitare, 12. 522 Columbus Ave
☎ 392-5800

Acorn Books, 96. 1436 Polk St
☎ 563-1736

Adorneme Umbrellas, 27. Crocker
Galleria, 50 Post St ☎ 397-4114

American Rag, 90. 1305 Van Ness
Ave ☎ 474-5214

Ann Taylor, 55.
240 Post St ☎ 788-0716

Another Time, 101. 1586 Market St
☎ 553-8900

Asakichi Japanese Antiques, 93.
Japan Center, 1730 Geary Blvd
☎ 921-2147

Automobilia, 88. 1701 Van Ness Ave
☎ 292-2710

B Dalton Bookseller, 26.
200 Kearny St ☎ 956-2850

Bally of Switzerland, 60.
238 Stockton St ☎ 398-7463

Barnes & Noble Booksellers, 8.
2552 Taylor St ☎ 292-6762

Banana Republic, 40.
256 Grant Ave ☎ 788-3087

Betsey Johnson, 65.
160 Geary St ☎ 398-2516

Betsey Johnson, 89.
2031 Fillmore St ☎ 567-2726

Birkenstock, 87.
1815 Polk St ☎ 776-5225

Borders Books & Music, 32.
400 Post St ☎ 399-1633

Bottega Veneta, 67.
108 Geary St ☎ 981-1700

Britex Fabrics, 66. 146 Geary St
☎ 392-2910

Brooks Brothers, 53.
201 Post St ☎ 397-4500

Capezio, 44. 126 Post St ☎ 421-5657

The Captain's Wharf, 84.
125 Powell St ☎ 391-2884

Chanel Boutique, 64.
155 Maiden La ☎ 981-1550

City Lights, 17.
261 Columbus Ave ☎ 362-8193

Clarion Music, 20. 816 Sacramento St
☎ 391-1317

**A Clean Well-Lighted Place For
Books, 97.** 601 Van Ness Ave
☎ 441-6670

The Coach Store, 51. 190 Post
St ☎ 392-1772

Columbus Books, 16.
540 Broadway ☎ 986-3872

Computown, 76.
710 Market St ☎ 956-8696

Crate & Barrel, 68.
125 Grant Ave ☎ 986-4000

Discount Camera, 69. 33 Kearny St
☎ 392-1100

Disney Store, 9. Pier 39 ☎ 391-4210

Disney Store, 32. 400 Post St
☎ 391-6866

Dragon House, 28. 455 Grant Ave
☎ 781-2351

Eastwind Books & Arts, 14. 1435
Stockton St ☎ 772-5899

Eddie Bauer, 57. 250 Post St
☎ 986-7600

Emporio Armani, 73. 1 Grant Ave
☎ 677-9400

Estee Lauder Services, Inc, 35.
360 Post St ☎ 616-3900

F. Dorian, 99.
388 Hayes St ☎ 861-3191

Fantasy, Etc, 95.
808 Larkin St ☎ 441-7617

FAO Schwarz Fifth Avenue, 77.
48 Stockton St ☎ 394-8700

Far East Fashions, 18.
953 Grant Ave ☎ 362-8171

**Frank's Fisherman's Supply,
Inc, 7.** 366 Jefferson St ☎ 775-1165

Gap, 82. 890 Market St ☎ 788-5909

Gap, 42. 100 Post St ☎ 421-2314

Gump's, 45. 135 Post St ☎ 982-1616

Headlines, 80.
838 Market St ☎ 956-4872

Hermès of Paris, 61.
212 Stockton St ☎ 391-7200

In-Wear Matinique, 50.
224 Grant Ave ☎ 391-6557

Jade Empire, 19.
832 Grant Ave ☎ 982-4498

Jaeger International Shop, 58.
272 Post St ☎ 421-3714

Jeffrey's Toys, 70.
7 3rd St ☎ 546-6551

Jet Age, 102. 250 Oak St ☎ 864-1950

Joan & David, 59.
1 Union Square ☎ 397-1958

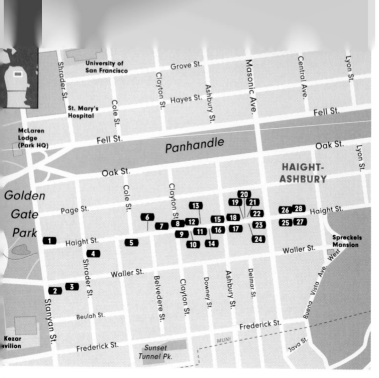

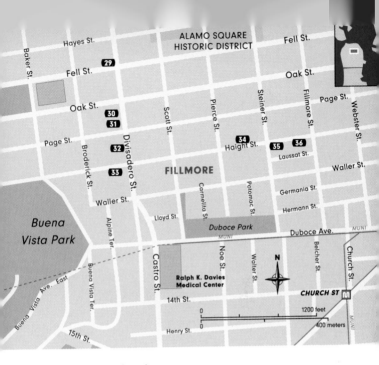

14th St.

Noe St.

Market St.

MUNI

CHURCH ST

M CHURCH ST

14th St.

17

18

Mission St.

BART

rona
ights

15th St.

Church St.

1

15th St.

Randall
Junior
Museum

Castro St.

Noe-Beaver
Mini-Park

2

16th St.

**Mission
Dolores**

16th ST **b**

BART

16th St.

7

4

MUNI (F)

3

19

Valencia St.

CASTRO ST

6

5

17th St.

**Mission
High School**

20

M

8

MUNI

9

10

Dolores St.

BART

11

18th St.

**EUREKA
VALLEY**

12

Eureka
Val. Rec.
Center

14 **13**

15 **16**

Castro St.

19th St.

**Mission
Dolores
Park**

Guerrero St.

21

Collingwood St.

20th St.

Diamond St.

21st St.

Sanchez St.

Church St.

Chattanooga St.

22

23

24

**MISSION
DISTRICT**

25

22nd St.

Alvardo St.

Noe St.

Alvarado
St.

23rd St.

MUNI

26

Elizabeth St.

28

27

Valencia St.

32

31

29

24th St.

33

Jersey St.

30

**NOE
VALLEY**

25th St.

Clipper St.

Castro St.

25th St.

26th St.

Dolores St.

Guerrero St.

Army St.

26th St.

Sanchez St.

26th St.

Army St.

Army St.

San Jose Ave.

27th St.

27th St.

Duncan St.

Tiffany Ave.

Mission St.

Duncan St.

Duncan St.

28th St.

Coleridge St.

Lundy's La.

Prospect Ave.

Valley St.

Castro St.

Noe St.

28th St.

Winfield St.

Sanchez St.

Upper Noe
Recreation
Center

29th St.

Day St.

BART

Guerrero St.

Elsie St.

N

M

30th St.

Chenery St.

Church St.

0   600 feet

0   200 meters

Randall St.

Reservoir

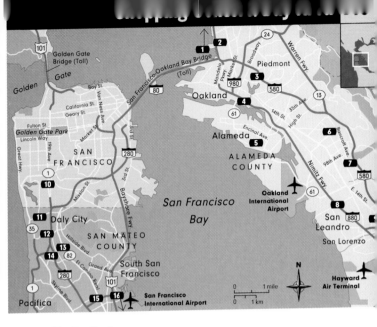

Listed by Site Number

1. El Cerrito Plaza
2. EmeryBay Public Mkt
3. Mac Arthur Bway Ctr
4. Jack London Village
5. South Shore Shopping Center
6. Eastmont Mall Shopping Center
7. Foothill Square Shopping Center
8. Marina Square
9. Bayfair Mall
10. Stonestown Galleria
11. Westlake Shopping Center
12. Saint Francis Square Shopping Center
13. 280 Metro Center
14. Serramonte Center
15. Tanforan Park Shopping Center
16. Stanford Shopping Center

Listed Alphabetically   Area Code (510) unless otherwise noted.

Bayfair Mall, 9. E 14th St and Fairmount Dr, San Leandro ☎ 357-6000

Eastmont Mall Shopping Center, 6. Hegenberger Expwy/Bancroft Ave, Oakland ☎ 632-1131

El Cerrito Plaza, 1. San Pablo Ave and Fairmont Blvd, El Cerrito ☎ 524-6535

EmeryBay Public Market, 2. Shellmound St and Christie Ave, Emeryville ☎ 652-9300

Foothill Square Shopping Center, 7. 10700 MacArthur Blvd, Oakland. ☎ 568-1494

Jack London Village, 4. 30 Jack London Sq, Oakland ☎ 893-7956

Mac Arthur Broadway Center, 3. 235 MacArthur Blvd, Oakland ☎ 658-0338

Marina Square, 8. Marina Blvd and I-880, San Leandro ☎ 523-8011

Saint Francis Sq Shopping Center, 12. 11 St Francis Sq, Daly City ☎ 650/992-9988

Serramonte Center, 14. Serramonte Blvd/I-280, Daly City ☎ 650/992-8686

South Shore Shopping Center, 5. Park St/I-880, Alameda ☎ 521-1515

Stanford Shopping Center, 16. El Camino Real & Page Mill Rd ☎ 650/617-8585

Stonestown Galleria, 10. 19th Ave and Winston Dr, SF ☎ 415/759-2626

Tanforan Park Shopping Center, 15. 1150 El Camino Real, San Bruno ☎ 650/873-2000

280 Metro Center, 13. Junipero Serra Blvd/I-280, Colma ☎ 415/474-6100

Westlake Shopping Center, 11. 285 Westlake Blvd and John Daly Blvd, Daly City ☎ 650/756-2161

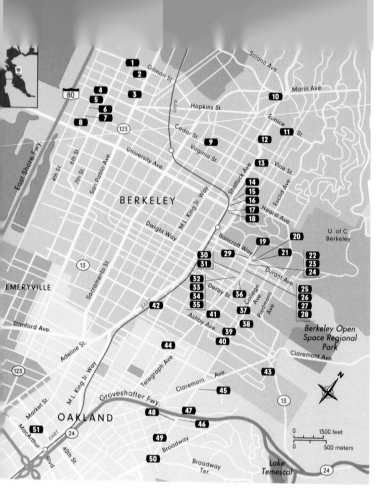

Listed by Site Number

Listed Alphabetically *Area Code (510) unless otherwise noted.*

BERKELEY

Amoeba Music, 30.
2455 Telegraph Ave ☎ 549-1125

Avant-Card, 20. 2580 Bancroft Way
☎ 644-2227

Bare Esentuals, 5. 1799 4th St
☎ 528-8025

Benetton, 29. 2387 Telegraph Ave
☎ 644-2221

Black Oak Books, 11.
1491 Shattuck Ave ☎ 486-0698

Body Time, 39. 2911 College Ave
☎ 845-2101

Body Time, 15. 1942 Shattuck Ave
☎ 841-5818

Body Time, 33. 2509 Telegraph Ave
☎ 548-3686

Buffalo Exchange, 36.
2512 Telegraph Ave ☎ 644-9202

Cody's Books, 26.
2454 Telegraph Ave ☎ 845-7852

Crate & Barrel Outlet, 6. 1785 4th St
☎ 528-5500

Futura, 23. 2350 Telegraph Ave
☎ 833-9050

Gaia Books Music & Crafts, 12. 1400
Shattuck Ave ☎ 548-4172

Games of Berkeley, 17.
2151 Shattuck Ave ☎ 540-7822

**Half-Price Books Records &
Magazines, 35.** 2525 Telegraph Ave
☎ 843-6412

Hear Music, 4. 1809 4th St
☎ 204-9595

Lhasa Karnak Herb Co., 14.
1938 Shattuck Ave ☎ 548-0372

Lhasa Karnak Herb Co., 34.
2513 Telegraph Ave ☎ 548-0380

**Looking Glass Photographers
Store, 41.** 2848 Telegraph Ave
☎ 548-6888

Marmot Mountain Works, 42. 3049
Adeline St ☎ 849-0735

Mars Mercantile, 24.
2398 Telegraph Ave ☎ 843-6711

Missing Link Bicycle Shop, 16.
1988 Shattuck Ave ☎ 843-4763

Moe's Books, 27. 2476 Telegraph Ave
☎ 849-2087

Movie Image, 18. 64 Shattuck Sq,
☎ 649-0296

The Nature Company, 8. 740 4th St
☎ 649-5448

New West, 40. 2967 College Ave
☎ 849-0701

Ninepatch, 10. 2001 Hopkins St
☎ 527-1700

Oak Barrel Winecraft Inc., 3.
1443 San Pablo Ave
☎ 849-0400

Pacific Bicycle, 37. 2701 College Ave
☎ 644-3751

Peet's Coffee & Tea, 13. 2124 Vine
Ave ☎ 841-0564

Peet's Coffee & Tea, 43. 2916
Domingo Ave ☎ 843-1434

Rasputin Music, 23. 2403 Telegraph
Ave ☎ 848-9005

Shakespeare & Co Books, 31.
2499 Telegraph Ave ☎ 841-8916

Shambala Booksellers, 28.
2482 Telegraph Ave ☎ 848-8443

Sharks, 32. 2505 Telegraph Ave
☎ 841-8736

Slash, 38. 2840 College Ave
☎ 841-7803

Smith & Hawken Outlet, 2. 1330 10th
St ☎ 525-2944

Subway Guitars, 9. 1800 Cedar St
☎ 841-4105

Tower Records Classical Annex, 21.
2518 Durant Ave ☎ 849-2500

Tower Records, 21. 2518 Durant Ave
☎ 841-0101

University Press Books, 19.
2430 Bancroft Way ☎ 548-0585

Urban Ore, 1. 7th & Gilman Sts
☎ 559-4450

X-Large, 25. 2422 Telegraph Ave
☎ 849-9242

Z Gallerie, 7. 1731 4th St ☎ 525-7591

OAKLAND

Crossroads Trading Co, 48. 5636
College Ave ☎ 420-1952

Deep Threads, 50. 5243 College Ave
☎ 653-4790

Madame Butterfly, 49.
5474 College Ave ☎ 653-1525

Mama Bears, 44.
6536 Telegraph Ave ☎ 428-9684

Marcus Books, 51. 3900 Martin Luther
King Jr. Way ☎ 652-2344

Market Hall, 46. 5655 College Ave
☎ 601-8208

Rockridge Rags, 47.
5711 College Ave ☎ 655-2289

Warm Things, 45. 6011 College Ave
☎ 428-9329

Lombard St.

Coit Tower

Greenwich St.

TELEGRAPH HILL

Filbert St.

Mason St.

Washington Square

Union St.

Taylor St.

The Embarcadero

Green St.

Davis St.

Front St.

Jones St.

Green St.

Columbus Ave.

Grant St.

Kearny St.

Montgomery St.

Sansome St.

Battery St.

RUSSIAN HILL

Coolbrith Park

Vallejo St.

Broadway Tunnel

Broadway

Pacific Ave.

Walton Park

Pacific Ave.

Jackson St.

SEE WASHINGTON SQUARE & COLUMBUS AVENUE AREA DETAIL MAP FOR NUMBERS 1–39

Leavenworth St.

Jackson St.

Cable Car Barn

Stockton St.

Portsmouth Square

CHINATOWN

Transamerica Pyramid

Washington St.

Clay St.

Drumm St.

Embarcadero Center

Sacramento St.

Washington St.

St. Mary's Square

EMBARCADERO

Clay St.

NOB HILL

Huntington Park

Sacramento St.

Grace Cathedral

California St.

Pine St.

Beale St.

Fremont St.

Jones St.

Pine St.

Bush St.

Powell St.

Mason St.

Market St.

BART/MUNI

Transbay Terminal

Taylor St.

Sutter St.

Crocker Galleria

MONTGOMERY ST

Union Square

Grant St.

Kearny St.

Post St.

Geary St.

Stockton St.

O'Farrell St.

Mission St.

Howard St.

2nd St.

Museum of Modern Art

Ellis St.

POWELL ST

Eddy St.

Jones St.

4th St.

3rd St.

Folsom St.

Moscone Convention Center

Hyde St.

Turk St.

Old U.S. Mint

Yerba Buena Square

Golden Gate Ave.

Market St.

Minna St.

5th St.

Howard St.

Ansel Adams Ctr.

Main Post Office

SOMA

Harrison St.

6th St.

CIVIC CENTER

Greyhound Bus Depot

4th St.

Mission St.

7th St.

Folsom St.

Bryant St.

S.F. Tennis Club

8th St.

CalTrain Depot

9th St.

Brannan St.

10th St.

Howard St.

Dore St.

Hall of Justice/ County Jail

CALTRAIN

Folsom St.

80

Mission Creek

Norfolk St.

Concourse Exhibition Center

11th St.

13th St.

Bryant St.

Dore St.

King St.

Berry St.

7th St.

280

6th St.

101

14th St.

Division St.

Alameda St.

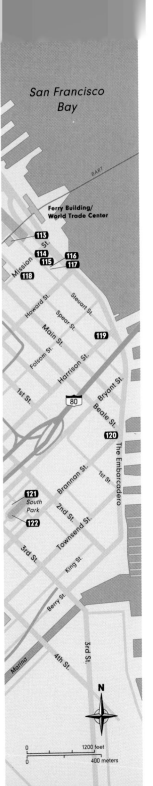

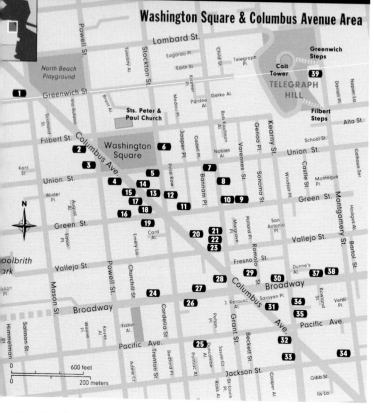

Listed by Site Number

Aioli, 92. 469 Bush St ☎ 249-0900. Mediterranean. $$

Albona Restaurant, 59. 545 Francisco St ☎ 441-1040. Eastern European. $$

Alfred's Steakhouse, 47. 695 Merchant St ☎ 781-7058. Steak. $$$

Anjou, 86. 44 Campton Pl ☎ 392-5373. French. $$$

Aqua, 107. 252 California St ☎ 956-9662. Seafood. $$$

Basil, 136. 1175 Folsom St ☎ 552-8999. Thai. $$

Basque Hotel and Restaurant, 29. 15 Romolo Pl ☎ 788-9404. Basque. $

Bella Voce, 61. Fairmont Hotel, 950 Mason St ☎ 772-5199. Italian. $-$$

The Big Four, 65. Huntington Hotel, 1075 California St ☎ 771-1140. Continental. $$-$$$

Big Nate's Barbecue, 141. 1665 Folsom St ☎ 861-4242. Barbecue. $

Bistro Roti, 116. 155 Steuart St ☎ 495-6500. French. $$

Bix, 46. 56 Gold St ☎ 433-6300. American. $$

Bizou, 128. 598 4th St ☎ 543-2222. Eclectic. $$

Bocce Café, 33. 478 Green St ☎ 981-2044. Italian. $$

Boulevard, 114. 1 Mission St ☎ 543-6084. American. $$$

Brainwash Café & Laundromat, 133. 1122 Folsom St ☎ 861-3663. American. $

Brandy Ho's, 37. 450 Broadway ☎ 362-6268. Chinese. $-$$

Buca Giovanni, 1. 800 Greenwich St ☎ 776-7766. Italian. $$

Burma House, 68. 720 Post St ☎ 775-1156. Burmese. $

Cadillac Bar, 132. 325 Minna St ☎ 543-8226. Mexican. $$

Café Bastille, 99. 22 Belden Pl ☎ 986-5673. French. $-$$

Café Claude, 97. 7 Claude La ☎ 392-3505. French. $

Café de la Presse, 93. 352 Grant Ave ☎ 398-2680. French/Mixed. $

Café 52, 102. 52 Belden Pl ☎ 433-5200. Mediterranean. $-$$

Café Jacqueline, 8. 1454 Grant Ave ☎ 981-5565. Souffles. $$

Café Tiramisu, 100. 28 Belden Pl ☎ 421-7044. Italian. $

Caffé Museo, 125. 151 3rd St ☎ 357-4500. Mediterrranean. $

Caffé Sport, 11. 574 Green St ☎ 981-1251. Italian Seafood. $$

Cafferata Restaurant, 2. 659 Columbus Ave ☎ 392-7544. Italian. $

California Pizza Kitchen, 77. 438 Geary St ☎ 563-8911. Californian. $

Calzone's, 20. 430 Columbus Ave ☎ 397-3600. Italian. $-$$

Campo Santo, 31. 240 Columbus Ave ☎ 433-9623. Mexican. $

Campton Place, 87. Campton Place Hotel, 340 Stockton St ☎ 955-5555. American. $$$-$$$$

Capp's Corner, 16. 1600 Powell St ☎ 989-2589. Italian. $

Carnelian Room, 103. 555 California St ☎ 433-7500. American. $$$

Charles Nob Hill, 57. 1250 Jones St ☎ 771-5400. Delicatessen. $-$$

China Moon Café, 69. 639 Post St ☎ 775-4789. California Chinese. $$

Cho-Cho, 35. 1020 Kearny St ☎ 397-3066. Japanese. $$

City of Paris, 84. 55 Geary St ☎ 441-4442. French. $-$$

Crown Room, 62. Fairmont Hotel, 850 Mason St ☎ 772-5131. American. $$$

Cypress Club, 34. 500 Jackson St ☎ 296-8555. American. $$$

David's Delicatessen, 76. 474 Geary St ☎ 771-1600. Delicatessen $-$$

Des Alpes, 24. 732 Broadway ☎ 788-9900. Basque. $

E & O Trading Company, 94. 314 Sutter St ☎ 693-0303. Pan-Asian. $$

Eleven, 138. 374 11th St ☎ 431-3337. Eclectic. $$-$$$

Emporio Armani Café, 83. 1 Grant Ave ☎ 677-9010. Italian. $-$$

Enrico's Sidewalk Café, 30. 504 Broadway ☎ 982-6223. Italian. $$

Farallon, 81. 450 Post St ☎ 956-6969. Seafood. $$$-$$$$

Listed Alphabetically (cont.)

Faz, 96. 161 Sutter St
☎ 362-0404. Middle Eastern.
$$

Fior d'Italia, 5. 601 Union St
☎ 986-1886. Italian. $-$$

Fleur de Lys, 67. 777 Sutter St
☎ 673-7779. French. $$$$

Fog City Diner, 40. 1300 Battery St
☎ 982-2000. American. $$

Fournou's Ovens, 63. 905 California
St ☎ 989-1910. American. $$$-$$$$

The French Room, 73.
Clift Hotel, 495 Geary St
☎ 775-4700. Californian. $$$$

Fringale, 129. 570 4th St
☎ 543-0573. French. $$

Garden Court, 123.
Market & New Montgomery Sts
☎ 392-8600. Continental. $$$

German Cook, 71. 612 O'Farrell St
☎ 776-9022. German. $

Gira Polli, 4. 659 Union St
☎ 434-4472. Italian. $

Globe, 44. 290 Pacific Ave
☎ 391-4132. Contemporary. $$$

The Gold Coast, 109. 230 California
St ☎ 989-6939. American. $$

Gold Mountain, 27. 644 Broadway
☎ 296-7733. Chinese. $-$$

The Gold Spike, 17. 527 Columbus
Ave ☎ 986-9747. Italian. $

Golden Dragon, 55. 816 Washington
St ☎ 398-3920. Chinese. $

Golden Dragon, 54. 822 Washington
St ☎ 398-4550. Chinese. $

Golden Phoenix, 51. 728 Washington
St ☎ 989-4400. Chinese. $-$$

**Gordon Biersch Brewery
Restaurant, 119.** 2 Harrison St
☎ 243-8246. Continental. $$

Grand Café, 72. Hotel Monaco, 501
Geary St ☎ 292-0101. Californian. $$

Hamburger Mary's, 139. 1582
Folsom St ☎ 626-1985. Burgers. $

Hang Ah Tea Room, 53. 1 Pagoda Pl
☎ 982-5686. Chinese. $

Harbor Village, 111. 4 Embarcadero
Center ☎ 781-8833. Chinese. $$

Harry Denton's, 117. 161 Steuart St
☎ 882-1333. American. $$

Hawthorne Lane, 126. 22 Hawthorne
St ☎ 777-9779. Contemporary. $$$

Helmand, 38. 430 Broadway
☎ 362-0641. Afghan. $

Historic John's Grill, 74. 63 Ellis St
☎ 986-0069. American. $$-$$$

House of Nanking, 33. 919 Kearny St
☎ 421-1429. Chinese. $

Hunan Restaurant, 43. 924 Sansome
St ☎ 956-7727. Chinese. $

Il Fornaio, 41. Levi's Plaza. 1265
Battery St ☎ 986-0100. Italian. $$

Il Pollaio, 15. 555 Columbus Ave
☎ 362-7727. Italian. $

Iron Horse, 85. 19 Maiden La
☎ 362-8133. Italian. $-$$

Jessie's, 137. 1256 Folsom St
☎ 437-2481. Cajun/Creole. $$

Julie's Supper Club, 134. 1123
Folsom St ☎ 861-0707. American. $$

Julius' Castle, 39. 1541 Montgomery
St ☎ 392-2222. French. $$$

Kamal Palace, 23. 641 Vallejo St
☎ 421-1132. Indian. $-$$

Kuleto's, 75. 221 Powell St
☎ 397-7720. Italian. $$

Kyo-ya, 124. Sheraton Palace Hotel,
2 New Montgomery St ☎ 546-5090.
Japanese. $$-$$$

La Bodega, 21. 1337 Grant Ave
☎ 433-0439. Spanish. $

La Scene Café & Bar, 78. 490 Geary
St ☎ 292-6430. American. $-$$

Le Central, 91. 453 Bush St
☎ 391-2233. French. $$

Le Charm, 131. 315 5th St
☎ 546-6128. French. $

**Longlife Noodle Company and
Jook Joint, 115.** 139 Steuart St
☎ 281-3818. Pan Asian. $

L'Osteria del Forno, 18. 519
Columbus Ave ☎ 982-1124.
Italian. $-$$

Lulu, 130. 816 Folsom St
☎ 495-5775. Mediterranean. $$

MacArthur Park, 45. 607 Front St
☎ 398-5700. American. $$

Manora, 140. 1600 Folsom St
☎ 861-6224. Thai. $

**Mario's Bohemian Cigar Store
Café, 14.** 566 Columbus Ave
☎ 362-0536. Italian. $

Masa's, 88. 648 Bush St
☎ 989-7154. French. $$$$

Maykadeh, 9. 470 Green St
☎ 362-8286. Persian. $$

Mo's, 22. 1322 Grant Ave
☎ 788-3779. American/Casual. $

Mon Kiang, 26. 683 Broadway
☎ 421-2015. Chinese. $

Moose's, 6. 1652 Stockton St
☎ 989-7800. Mediterranean. $$-$$$

New Asia, 25. 772 Pacific Ave
☎ 391-6666. Chinese/Dim Sum. $

North Beach Pizza, 7. 1499 Grant Ave
☎ 433-2444. Italian. $

North Beach Restaurant, 12. 1512
Stockton St ☎ 392-1700. Italian.
$$-$$$

One Market, 113. 1 Market St
☎ 777-5577. American. $$$

**O'Reilly Irish Pub and Restaurant,
19.** 622 Green St ☎ 989-6222.
Irish. $$

Palio d'Asti, 104. 640 Sacramento St
☎ 395-9800. Italian. $$-$$$

Pan Pacific Grill, 80.
Pan Pacific Hotel, 500 Post St
☎ 929-2087. Californian. $$-$$$

Park Grill, 106. Park Hyatt Hotel,
333 Battery St ☎ 296-2933.
Continental. $-$$

Pazzia, 127. 337 3rd St ☎ 512-1693.
Pizza. $-$$

Pickled Ginger, 120. 100 Brannan St
☎ 977-1230. Pan Asian/American. $$

Plouf, 101. 40 Belden St ☎ 986-6491.
French. $$

Postrio, 79. 545 Post St
☎ 776-7825. American. $$$-$$$$

R & G Lounge, 52. 631 Kearny St
☎ 982-7877. Chinese. $-$$

Ristorante Ecco, 122. 101 South Park
☎ 495-3291. Italian. $$

**Ritz-Carlton Dining Room &
Terrace, 89.** 600 Stockton St
☎ 296-7465. American. $$$-$$$$

Rose Pistola, 13. 532 Columbus Ave
☎ 399-0499. Italian. $$

Rubicon, 105. 558 Sacramento St
☎ 434-4100. Modern French. $$$

Rumpus, 95. 1 Tillman Pl
☎ 421-2300. Contemporary Bistro. $$

Sam's Grill 98. 374 Bush St
☎ 421-0594. Seafood. $$-$$$

San Francisco Brewing Co, 32. 155
Columbus Ave ☎ 434-3344.
American. $

Sanraku, 66. 704 Sutter St
☎ 771-0803. Japanese. $-$$

The Savoy Brasserie, 70.
580 Geary St ☎ 474-8686.
French. $$

**Scott's Seafood Grill & Bar,
110.** 3 Embarcadero Center
☎ 981-0622. Seafood. $$-$$$

Sears Fine Foods, 82. 439 Powell St
☎ 986-1160. Coffee Shop. $

South Park Café, 121. 108 South Park
Ave ☎ 495-7275. French. $$

Splendido, 112. 4 Embarcadero Ctr
☎ 986-3222. Mediterranean. $$-$$$

The Stinking Rose, 28. 325 Columbus
Ave ☎ 781-7673. Garlic. $$

Tadich Grill, 108. 240 California St
☎ 391-1849. Seafood. $$-$$$

Tommaso's, 36. 1042 Kearny St
☎ 398-9696. Italian. $-$$

**Tommy Toy's Haute Cuisine
Chinoise, 50.** 655 Montgomery St
☎ 397-4888. Chinese. $$-$$$

Top of the Mark, 64.
Mark Hopkins Hotel, 1 Nob Hill
☎ 392-3434. American. $$$

Up & Down Club, 135. 1151 Folsom St
☎ 626-2388. Eclectic American. $-$$

Venticello Restaurant, 56.
1257 Taylor St ☎ 922-2545. Italian. $$

Vertigo, 49. 600 Montgomery St
☎ 433-7250. Mediterranean. $$$

Washington Sq Bar and Grill, 3.
1707 Powell St ☎ 982-8123. Italian. $$

Waterfront Restaurant, 42.
Pier 7, Embarcadero
☎ 391-2696. Seafood. $$-$$$

Wu Kong, 118. 101 Spear St
☎ 957-9300. Chinese. $$

Yamato, 90. 717 California St
☎ 397-3456. Japanese. $-$$

Yank Sing, 48. 427 Battery St
☎ 326-1640. Chinese. $

Zarzuela, 58. 2000 Hyde St
☎ 346-0800. Spanish. $$

Zax, 60. 2330 Taylor St ☎ 563-6266.
Contemporary American/Eclectic. $$

$$$$ = over $50 $$$ = $30–$50 $$ = $20–$30 $ = under $20
Based on cost per person, excluding drinks, service, and 8.5% sales tax.

MAP 43 Restaurants/Marina, Pacific Heights,

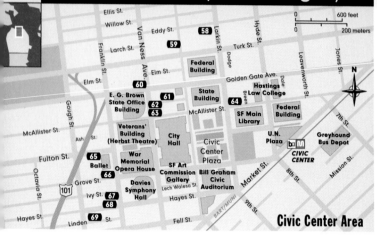

Civic Center Area

Listed Alphabetically   Area Code (415) unless otherwise noted.

Acquarello, 49. 1722 Sacramento St
☎ 567–5432. Italian. $$–$$$

Ba Le, 57. 511 Jones St ☎ 474–7270.
Vietnamese. $

Backflip, 58. Phoenix Hotel,
601 Eddy St. ☎ 415/771–3547.
American/Eclectic. $$

Bahia Cabana, 71. 1600 Market St
☎ 626–3306. Brazilian. $–$$

Balboa Cafe, 11. 3199 Fillmore St
☎ 921–3944. American. $$

Bistro Aix, 3. 3340 Steiner St
☎ 202–0100. French. $–$$

Bistro Clovis, 70. 1596 Market St
☎ 864–0231. French. $

Blue Light Cafe, 22. 1979 Union St
☎ 922–5510. Southwestern. $–$$

Café de Paris, 20. 2032 Union St
☎ 931–5006. French. $–$$$

Café Marimba, 6. 2317 Chestnut St
☎ 776–1506. Mexican. $$

Caffe delle Stelle, 69. 395 Hayes St
☎ 252–1110. Italian. $$$

California Culinary Academy, 59.
625 Polk St ☎ 771–3500. French. $$–$$$

Cassis Bistro, 14. 2120 Greenwich St
☎ 292–0770. French. $–$$

Couscous Morocco, 19. 2165 Union St
☎ 563–9638. Moroccan. $–$$

Crustacean, 52. 1475 Polk St
☎ 776–2722. Vietnamese. $$–$$$

Doidge's Kitchen, 18. 2217 Union St
☎ 921–2149. Breakfast. $

Elite Cafe, 29. 2049 Fillmore St
☎ 346–8668. Cajun/Creole. $$$

Ella's, 26. 500 Presidio Ave
☎ 441–5669. American/Breakfast. $$

Frascati, 43. 1901 Hyde St
☎ 928–1406. Italian. $$–$$$

Gaylord's, 41. Ghirardelli Sq
☎ 771–8822. Indian. $$–$$$

German Cook, 56. 612 O'Farrell St
☎ 776–9022. German. $

Greens, 1. Fort Mason, Bldg A
☎ 771–6222. Vegetarian. $$–$$$

The Grubstake Restaurant, 53.
1525 Pine St ☎ 673–8268. Diner. $

Hard Rock Cafe, 50. 1699 Van Ness
Ave ☎ 885–1699. American. $

Harris', 45. 2100 Van Ness Ave
☎ 673-1888. Steakhouse. $$$

Harry's On Fillmore, 30.
2020 Fillmore St ☎ 921-1000.
American. $-$$

Hayes Street Grill, 68. 320 Hayes St
☎ 863-5545. Seafood. $$-$$$

Home Plate, 5. 2274 Lombard St
☎ 922-4663. American. $

House Of Prime Rib, 47. 1906 Van
Ness Ave ☎ 885-4605. Steak. $$-$$$

**Hyde Street Seafood House and
Raw Bar, 46.** 1509 Hyde St
☎ 931-3474. Seafood. $

Izzy's Steak & Chop House, 4. 3345
Steiner St ☎ 563-0487. Steakhouse. $$

Jackson Fillmore Trattoria, 23. 2506
Fillmore St ☎ 346-5288. Italian. $$

Jardinière, 66. 300 Grove St
☎ 861-5555. Contemporary
American/Eclectic. $$$

Juban, 35. 1581 Webster St
☎ 776-5822. Japanese. $$

Kushi Tsuru, 37. 1737 Post St
☎ 922-9902. Japanese. $-$$

La Folie, 44. 2316 Polk St
☎ 776-5577. French. $$$-$$$$

Lhasa Moon, 9. 2420 Lombard St
☎ 674-9898. Tibetan. $

Liverpool Lil's, 15. 2942 Lyon St
☎ 921-6664. English. $

Maharani Restaurant, 54. 1122 Post St
☎ 775-1988. Indian. $-$$

Maki, 34. 1825 Post St ☎ 921-5215.
Japanese. $$

Max's Opera Cafe, 60. 601 Van
Ness Ave ☎ 771-7301. American. $-$$

McCormick & Kuleto's, 42. 900 North
Point St ☎ 929-1730. Seafood.
$$-$$$

The Meetinghouse, 31. 1701 Octavia St.
☎ 922-6733. Contemporary
American/Electic. $$

Mifune, 36. Japan Center, 1737 Post St
☎ 922-0337. Japanese. $

Millenium, 64. 246 McAllister
☎ 487-9800. Vegetarian. $$

New Korea House, 39. 1620 Post St
☎ 931-7834. Korean. $$

Nightshade, 32. 2101 Sutter St
☎ 541-0795. Mediterranean/Pizza.
$-$$

North India, 13. 3131 Webster St
☎ 931-1556. Indian. $$

Oritalia, 28. 1915 Fillmore St
☎ 346-1333. Oriental/Italian. $$

Ovation, 65. Inn at the Opera,
333 Fulton St ☎ 553-8100.
American/Eclectic. $$$

Pane e Vino, 16. 3011 Steiner St
☎ 346-2111. Italian. $$-$$$

Pasta Pomodoro, 2. 2027 Chestnut St
☎ 474-3400. Italian. $

Pauli's Cafe, 24. 2500 Washington St
☎ 921-5159. American. $

Perry's, 21. 1944 Union St
☎ 922-9022. American. $$

PlumpJack Café, 12. 3201 Fillmore St
☎ 463-4755. Mediterranean. $$-$$$

**Rasselas Ethiopian Cuisine and
Jazz Club, 27.** 2801 California St
☎ 567-5010. Ethiopian. $$$

Ristorante Parma, 10. 3314 Steiner St
☎ 567-0500. Italian. $-$$

Rose's Café, 17. 2298 Union St
☎ 775-2200. Mediterranean. $-$$

Sanppo, 33. 1702 Post St
☎ 346-3486. Japanese. $

Scott's Seafood Grill, 8. 2400
Lombard St ☎ 563-8988. Seafood. $$

Spuntino, 62. 524 Van Ness Ave
☎ 861-7772. Italian. $

Stars, 61. 150 Redwood St
☎ 861-7827. American. $$$

Stars Café, 63. 500 Van Ness Ave
☎ 861-4344. American. $-$$

Suppenkuche, 40. 601 Hayes St
☎ 252-9289. German. $-$$

Sushi-A, 38. 1737 Buchanan St
☎ 931-4685. Japanese/Sushi. $$

Swan Oyster Depot, 51. 1517 Polk St
☎ 673-1101. Seafood. $$

Thai Spice, 48. 1730 Polk St
☎ 775-4777. Thai. $

Tommy's Joynt, 55. 1101 Geary St
☎ 775-4216. American. $

Vicolo, 67. 150 Ivy St
☎ 863-2382. Pizza. $

Vivande Porta Via, 25. 2125 Fillmore
St ☎ 346-4430. Italian. $$$

Zinzino, 7. 2355 Chestnut St
☎ 346-6623. Italian. $$

Zuni Cafe & Grill, 72. 1658 Market St
☎ 552-2522. American. $$-$$$

$$$$ = *over $50* $$$ = *$30-$50* $$ = *$20-$30* $ = *under $20*
Based on cost per person, excluding drinks, service, and 8.5% sales tax.

MAP 44 Restaurants/Sunset, Richmond &

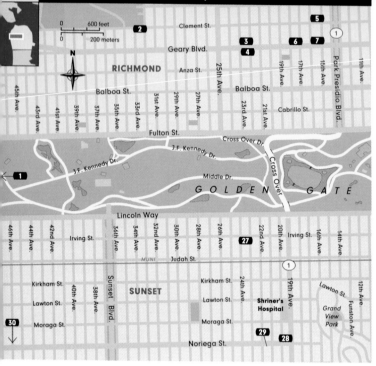

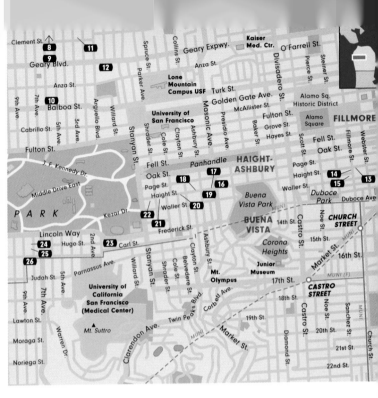

$$$$ = over $50 $$$ = $30-$50 $$ = $20-$30 $ = under $20
Based on cost per person, excluding drinks, service, and 8.5% sales tax.

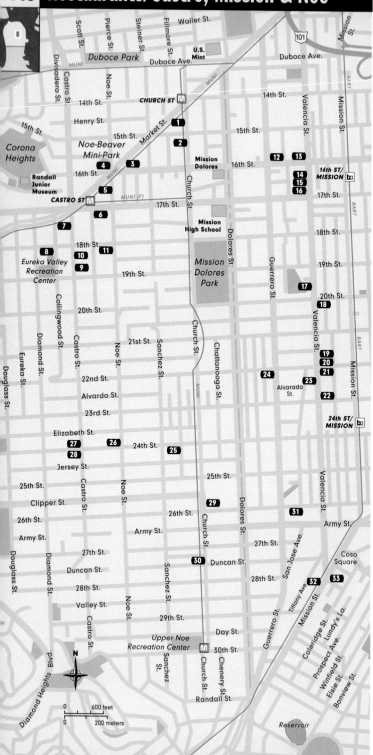

Listed Alphabetically   Area Code (415) unless otherwise noted.

Amira, 16. 590 Valencia St ☎ 621-6213. Middle Eastern. $–$$

Anchor Oyster Bar, 9. 579 Castro St ☎ 431-3990. Seafood. $$

Bagdad Cafe, 3. 2295 Market St ☎ 621-4434. Diner. $

Boogaloos, 20. 3296 22nd St ☎ 824-3211. Breakfast. $

Dusit, 33. 3221 Mission St ☎ 826-4639. Thai. $–$$

El Zocalo, 32. 3230 Mission St ☎ 282-2572. Salvadoran. $

Esperpento, 21. 3295 22nd St ☎ 282-8867. Tapas. $–$$

The Flying Saucer, 24. 1000 Guerrero St ☎ 641-9955. Californian. $$$

Haystack Pizza, 25. 3881 24th St ☎ 647-1929. Italian. $

Hot n' Hunky, 11. 4039 18th St ☎ 621-6365. Burgers. $

La Méditerranée, 4. 288 Noe St ☎ 431-7210. Mediterranean. $

La Rondalla, 18. 901 Valencia St ☎ 647-7474. Mexican. $–$$

Little Italy Ristorante, 28. 4109 24th St ☎ 821-1515. Italian. $–$$

Ma Tante Sumi, 8. 4243 18th St ☎ 626-7864. French/Nouvelle. $$–$$$

Nippon (No Name) Sushi, 2. 314 Church St. Sushi. $–$$

Orphan Andy's, 6. 3991 17th St ☎ 864-9795. Diner. $

Panos', 26. 4000 24th St ☎ 824-8000. Californian. $–$$

Pastaio, 12. 3182 16th St ☎ 255-2440. Italian. $–$$

Patio Café, 10. 531 Castro St ☎ 621-4640. American. $

Pozole, 5. 2337 Market St ☎ 626-2666. Mexican. $

Radio Valencia, 22. 1199 Valencia St ☎ 826-1199. American. $

Rami's Caffé & Patio, 28. 1361 Church St ☎ 641-0678. Mediterranean. $

The Slanted Door, 15. 584 Valencia St ☎ 861-8032. Vietnamese. $–$$

Saigon Saigon, 23. 1132 Valencia St ☎ 206-9635. Vietnamese. $

Scenic India, 14. 532 Valencia St ☎ 621-7226. Indian. $–$$

Sparky's 24 Hour Diner, 1. 242 Church St ☎ 621-6001. Diner/Pizza. $

Speckmann's, 30. 1550 Church St ☎ 282-0565. German. $$

Thailand Restaurant, 7. 438 Castro St ☎ 863-6868. Thai. $

Ti Couz, 13. 3108 16th St ☎ 252-7373. Crepes. $

Timo's, 17. 842 Valencia St ☎ 647-0558. Tapas. $–$$

Tom Peasant Pies, 27. 4108 24th St ☎ 642-1316. Savory Pies. $

We Be Sushi, 19. 1071 Valencia St ☎ 826-0607. Sushi. $

Yuet Lee Seafood, 31. 3601 26th St ☎ 550-8998. Chinese. $

$$$$ = over $50 $$$ = $30–$50 $$ = $20–$30 $ = under $20
Based on cost per person, excluding drinks, service, and 8.5% sales tax.

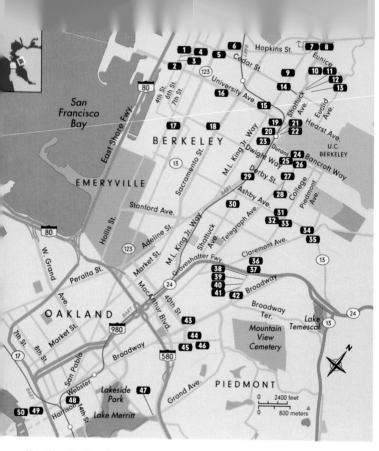

Listed by Site Number

$$$$ = over $50 $$$ = $30–$50 $$ = $20–$30 $ = under $20

Based on cost per person, excluding drinks, service, and 8.5% sales tax.

Barney's Gourmet Burgers, 36. 5819 College Ave ☎ 601-0444. Burgers. $

Barney's Gourmet Burgers, 20. 1600 Shattuck Ave ☎ 849-2827. Burgers. $

Barney's Gourmet Burgers, 46. 4162 Piedmont Ave ☎ 655-7180. Burgers. $

Bateau Ivre, 28. 2629 Telegraph Ave ☎ 849-1100. French. $$

Bay Wolf, 45. 3853 Piedmont Ave ☎ 655-6004. Californian. $$-$$$

Bette's Ocean View Diner, 1. 1807 4th St ☎ 644-3230. American. $

The Blue Nile, 27. 2525 Telegraph Ave ☎ 540-6777. Ethiopian. $

Cactus Taqueria, 39. 5525 College Ave ☎ 547-1305. Mexican. $

Café de la Paz, 14. 1600 Shattuck Ave ☎ 843-0662. Latin American. $-$$

Café Fanny, 5. 1603 San Pablo Ave ☎ 524-5447. Sandwiches. $

Café Intermezzo, 25. 2442 Telegraph Ave ☎ 849-4592. Sandwiches/Salads. $

Café Venezia, 15. 1799 University Ave ☎ 849-4681. Italian. $-$$

Cancun Taqueria, 22. 2134 Allston Way ☎ 549-0964. Mexican. $

Cha-Am, 12. 1543 Shattuck Ave 848-9664. Thai. $

Chester's Café, 13. 1508 Walnut St ☎ 849-9995. American. $

Chez Panisse Restaurant and Café, 11. 1517 Shattuck Ave ☎ 548-5525. Californian. $$$-$$$$

China Station, 2. 700 University Ave ☎ 548-7880. Chinese. $

Citron, 41. 5484 College Ave ☎ 653-5484. Nouvelle. $$-$$$

Creme de la Creme, 42. 5362 College Ave ☎ 420-8822. Country French. $$-$$$

Espresso Roma, 32. 2960 Ashby Ave ☎ 644-3773. Sandwiches/Coffee. $

Fatapple's, 9. 1346 M L King Jr Way ☎ 526-2260. Burgers/American. $

Flint's Bar-B-Q, 30. 6609 Shattuck Ave ☎ 653-0593. Barbecue. $

Ginger Island, 4. 1820 4th St ☎ 644-0444. Vietnamese. $$

The Homemade Café, 18. 2454 Sacramento St ☎ 845-1940. Breakfast. $

Juan's Place, 17. 941 Carlton St ☎ 845-6904. Mexican. $

King Yen, 33. 2995 College Ave ☎ 845-1286. Chinese. $-$$

King Yen, 44. 4080 Piedmont Ave ☎ 652-9678. Chinese. $-$$

Kirala, 29. 2100 Ward St ☎ 549-3486. Japanese/Sushi. $$

La Méditerranée, 31. 2936 College Ave ☎ 540-7773. Mediterranean. $

Lalime's Café, 6. 1329 Gilman St ☎ 527-9838. Mediterranean. $$

Mama's Royal Café, 43. 4012 Broadway ☎ 547-7600. Breakfast. $

Musical Offering Café, 24. 2430 Bancroft Way ☎ 849-0211. Gourmet Sandwiches/Salads. $

Oakland Grill, 49. 3rd & Franklin Sts ☎ 835-1176. American. $

Oliveto Café & Restaurant, 38. 5655 College Ave ☎ 547-5356. Italian. $$$

Panini, 21. 2115 Allston Way ☎ 849-0405. Gourmet Sandwiches. $

Pasand Madras Cuisine, 23. 2286 Shattuck Ave ☎ 549-2559. Indian. $-$$

Pho-84, 48. 416 13th St ☎ 832-1429. Vietnamese. $

Plearn, 19. 2050 University Ave ☎ 841-2148. Thai. $-$$

Rick and Ann's, 35. 2922 Domingo Ave ☎ 649-8538. American. $-$$

Rivoli, 7. 1539 Solano Ave ☎ 526-2542. Californian/Mediterranean. $$

Rockridge Café, 40. 5492 College Ave ☎ 653-1567. American. $

Santa Fe Bar and Grill, 16. 1310 University Ave ☎ 841-4740. Southwestern. $$-$$$

Saul's Delicatessen, 10. 1475 Shattuck Ave ☎ 848-3354. Deli. $

Spenger's Fish Grotto, 3. 1919 4th St ☎ 845-7771. Seafood. $$

Thai House, 26. 2511 Channing Way ☎ 843-7352. Thai. $

Viva Taqueria, 34. Russell St & Claremont Ave ☎ 843-5565. Mexican. $

Yoshi's, 50. 510 Embacadero West ☎ 238-9200. Japanese. $$

Zachary's Chicago Pizza, 8. 1853 Solano Ave ☎ 525-5950. Pizza. $

Zachary's Chicago Pizza, 37. 5801 College Ave ☎ 655-6385. Pizza. $

Zza's Trattoria, 47. 552 Grand Ave ☎ 839-9124. Italian. $

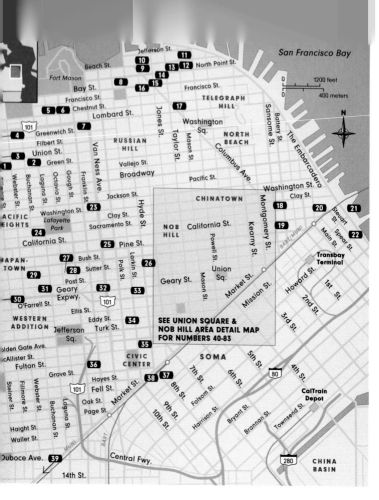

The Mansions, 24.
2220 Sacramento St
☎ 929-9444. 📠 567-9391. $$$

Marina Inn, 5. 3110 Octavia St
☎ 928-1000. 📠 928-5909. $

Mark Hopkins Inter-Continental, 43.
999 California St
☎ 392-3434. 📠 421-3302. $$$$

The Maxwell, 76. 386 Geary St
☎ 986-2000. 📠 397-2447. $$

Miyako Inn-Best Western, 29.
1800 Sutter St ☎ 921-4000.
📠 923-1064. $$

Nikko Hotel San Francisco, 82.
222 Mason St ☎ 394-1111.
📠 394-1106. $$$$

Nob Hill Lambourne, 46.
725 Pine St ☎ 433-2287. 📠 433-0975.
$$$$

Pan Pacific Hotel, 65.
500 Post St ☎ 771-8600. 📠 398-0267.
$$$$

Park Hyatt San Francisco, 18.
333 Battery St ☎ 392-1234.
📠 421-2433. $$$$

Petite Auberge, 52. 863 Bush St
☎ 928-6000. 📠 775-5717. $$

Phoenix Hotel, 34. 601 Eddy St
☎ 776-1380. 📠 885-3109. $$

Powell Hotel, 83. 28 Cyril Magnin St
☎ 398-3200. 📠 398-3654. $$-$$$

Prescott Hotel, 67. 545 Post St
☎ 563-0303. 📠 563-6831. $$$$

The Queen Anne, 27. 1590 Sutter St
☎ 441-2828. 📠 775-5212. $$-$$$$

Radisson Miyako Hotel, 31. 1625
Post St ☎ 922-3200. 📠 921-0417. $$$

**Ramada Hotel-Fisherman's Wharf,
15.** 590 Bay St ☎ 885-4700.
📠 771-8945. $$-$$$$

Ramada Hotel-Civic Center, 38.
1231 Market St ☎ 626-8000.
📠 861-1460. $$$

Ramada Inn at Union Square, 81.
345 Taylor St ☎ 673-2332.
📠 398-0733. $$$

**Renaissance Stanford Court Hotel,
44.** 905 California St
☎ 989-3500. 📠 391-0513. $$$$

Ritz-Carlton San Francisco, 45.
600 Stockton St ☎ 296-7465.
📠 291-0288. $$$$

**San Francisco Hilton and
Towers, 80.** 333 O'Farrell St
☎ 771-1400. 📠 771-6807. $$$$

San Francisco Marriott, 59.
55 4th St ☎ 896-1600. 📠 896-6177.
$$$$

**San Francisco Marriott-Fisherman's
Wharf, 16.** 1250 Columbus Ave
☎ 775-7555. 📠 474-2099. $$$-$$$$

San Remo Hotel, 17. 2237 Mason St
☎ 776-8688. 📠 776-2811. $

Savoy, 69. 580 Geary St
☎ 441-2700. 📠 441-2700. $$$

Seal Rock Inn, 30.
545 Point Lobos Ave
☎ 752-8000. 📠 752-6034. $-$$

Shannon Court, 70. 550 Geary St
☎ 775-5000. 📠 775-9388. $$$

Sheraton at Fisherman's Wharf, 12.
2500 Mason St ☎ 362-5500.
📠 956-5275. $$$-$$$$

Sheraton Palace, 57.
2 New Montgomery St
☎ 392-8600. 📠 543-0671. $$$$

Sherman House, 1. 2160 Green St
☎ 563-3600. 📠 563-1882. $$$$

Sir Francis Drake, 62. 450 Powell St
☎ 392-7755. 📠 395-8599. $$$

Town House Motel, 6.
1650 Lombard St
☎ 885-5163. 📠 771-9889. $

**Travelodge at Fisherman's Wharf,
11.** 250 Beach St
☎ 392-6700. 📠 986-7853. $$

Tuscan Inn, 13. 425 North Point St
☎ 561-1100. 📠 561-1199. $$$

Union Street Inn, 3. 2229 Union St
☎ 346-0424. 📠 922-8046. $$$

Vintage Court, 49. 650 Bush St
☎ 392-4666. 📠 433-4065. $$$

Warwick Regis Hotel, 72.
490 Geary St ☎ 928-7900.
📠 441-8788. $$$-$$$$

Westin St Francis, 77. 335 Powell St
☎ 397-7000. 📠 774-0124. $$$$

White Swan Inn, 51. 845 Bush St
☎ 775-1755. 📠 775-5717. $$$

York Hotel, 26. 940 Sutter St
☎ 885-6800. 📠 885-2115. $$$

$$$$ = *over $175* $$$ = *$120-$175* $$ = *$80-$120* $ = *under $80*
All prices are for a standard double room, excluding 12% room tax.

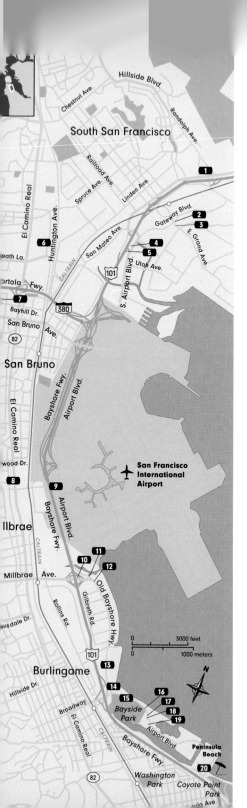

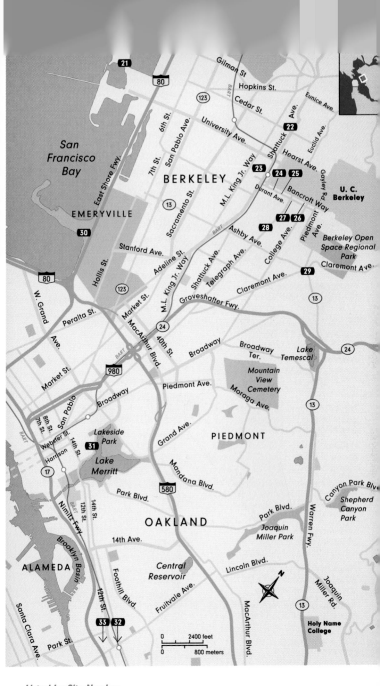

Listed Alphabetically   *Area Code (650) unless otherwise noted.*

AIRPORT

Clarion Hotel, 10.
401 E Millbrae Ave, Millbrae
☎ 692-6363. ⚞ 697-8735.
$$-$$$

Comfort Inn, 8. 1390 El Camino Real,
Millbrae ☎ 952-3200. ⚞ 952-7796. $$

Comfort Suites, 3. 121 E Grand Ave,
South SF ☎ 589-7766. ⚞ 589-2231. $$

Courtyard by Marriott, 7.
1050 Bayhill Dr, San Bruno
☎ 952-3333. ⚞ 952-4707. $$-$$$

Embassy Suites, 2.
250 Gateway Blvd, South SF
☎ 589-3400. ⚞ 876-0305. $$$

**Embassy Suites-San Francisco
Airport/Burlingame, 18.**
150 Anza Blvd, Burlingame
☎ 342-4600. ⚞ 343-8137. $$$

Days Inn Airport North, 1.
1113 Airport Blvd, South SF
☎ 873-9300. ⚞ 873-6200. $$

**Doubletree Hotel San Francisco
Airport, 16.** 835 Airport Blvd, Burlingame
☎ 344-5500. ⚞ 340-8851. $$$

**Holiday Inn Crown Plaza-San
Francisco Airport, 19.**
600 Airport Blvd, Burlingame
☎ 340-8500. ⚞ 343-1546. $$-$$$$

**Holiday Inn San Francisco Airport
North, 5.** 275 S Airport Blvd, South SF
☎ 873-3550. ⚞ 873-4524. $-$$$$

**Hyatt Regency San Francisco
Airport, 13.** 1333 Old Bayshore Hwy,
Burlingame ☎ 347-1234.
⚞ 696-2669. $$-$$$$

La Quinta Motor Inn, 20.
20 Airport Blvd, South SF
☎ 583-2223. ⚞ 589-6770. $$

Plaza Park Hotel, 15. 1177 Airport
Blvd, Burlingame ☎ 342-9200.
⚞ 342-1655. $$-$$$

**Ramada Inn San Francisco Airport
North, 4.** 245 S Airport Blvd, South SF
☎ 589-7200. ⚞ 588-5007. $$-$$$

Ramada on the Bay, 14.
1250 Old Bayshore Hwy, Burlingame
☎ 347-2381. ⚞ 348-8838. $$-$$$

Red Roof Inn, 17. 777 Airport Blvd,
Burlingame ☎ 342-7772. ⚞ 342-2635.
$-$$

San Francisco Airport Hilton, 9.
SF International Airport
☎ 589-0770. ⚞ 589-4696. $$$$

San Francisco Airport Marriott, 12.
1800 Old Bayshore Hwy, Burlingame
☎ 692-9100. ⚞ 692-8016. $$-$$$$

**Summerfield Suites Hotel San
Francisco Airport, 6.**
1350 Huntington Ave, San Bruno
☎ 588-0770. ⚞ 588-0892. $$$$

**Westin Hotel San Francisco
Airport, 11.** 1 Old Bayshore Hwy,
Millbrae ☎ 692-3500. ⚞ 872-8111. $$$

EAST BAY

The Bancroft Hotel, 26.
2680 Bancroft Way, Berkeley
☎ 510/549-1000. ⚞ 510/549-1070. $-$$

The Beau Sky Hotel, 27.
2520 Durant Ave, Berkeley
☎ 510/540-7688. ⚞ 510/540-8089.
$-$$

The Berkeley City Club, 24.
2315 Durant Ave, Berkeley
☎ 510/848-7800. ⚞ 510/848-5900. $$

Berkeley Marina Marriott, 21.
200 Marina Blvd, Berkeley
☎ 510/548-7920. ⚞ 510/548-7944. $$$

Claremont Resort and Spa, 29.
Ashby & Domingo Aves, Oakland
☎ 510/843-3000. ⚞ 510/549-8582. $$$$

Clarion Suites Lake Merritt, 31. 1800
Madison St, Oakland ☎ 510/832-2300.
⚞ 510/832-7150. $$$

The French Hotel, 22. 1538 Shattuck
Ave, Berkeley ☎ 510/548-9930.
⚞ 510/548-9930. $$-$$$

Gramma's Rose Garden Inn, 28.
2740 Telegraph Ave, Berkeley
☎ 510/549-2145. ⚞ 510/549-1085.
$$-$$$

Holiday Inn Bay Bridge, 30. 1800
Powell St, Emeryville ☎ 510/658-9300.
⚞ 510/547-8166. $$$

Holiday Inn Oakland Airport, 32.
500 Hegenberger Rd, Oakland
☎ 510/562-5311. ⚞ 510/636-1539. $$

Hotel Durant, 25. 2600 Durant Ave,
Berkeley ☎ 510/845-8981.
⚞ 510/486-8336. $$$

Hotel Shattuck, 23. 2086 Allston
Way, Berkeley ☎ 510/845-7300.
⚞ 510/644-2088. $$

Oakland Airport Hilton, 33.
1 Hegenberger Rd, Oakland
☎ 510/635-5000. ⚞ 510/568-3362.
$$$

$$$$ = over $175 $$$ = $120-$175 $$ = $80-$120 $ = under $80
All prices are for a standard double room, excluding 12% room tax.

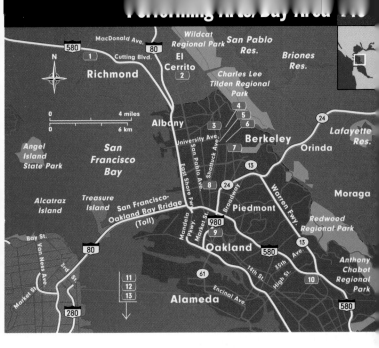

Listed by Site Number

EAST BAY

1 Masquers Playhouse
2 Contra Costa Civic Theatre
3 Live Oak Theatre
4 La Val's Subterranean
5 Berkeley Repertory Theatre
6 Zellerbach Playhouse
7 Julia Morgan Theatre
8 Black Repertory Group
9 Paramount Theatre
10 Mills College Theatre

SOUTH BAY

11 Mountain View Center for the Performing Arts
12 Burgess Theater
13 Villa Montalvo Center for the Arts

Listed Alphabetically   Area Code (510) unless otherwise noted.

EAST BAY

Berkeley Repertory Theatre, 5. 2025 Addison St, Berkeley ☎ 845-4700

Black Repertory Group, 8. 3201 Adeline St, Berkeley ☎ 652-2120

Contra Costa Civic Theatre, 2. 951 Pomona Ave, El Cerrito ☎ 524-9132

Julia Morgan Theatre, 7. 2640 College Ave, Berkeley ☎ 845-8542

La Val's Subterranean, 4. 1834 Euclid Ave, Berkeley ☎ 843-5617

Live Oak Theatre, 3. 1301 Shattuck Ave, Berkeley ☎ 841-5580

Masquers Playhouse, 1. 105 Park Place, Point Richmond ☎ 232-4031

Mills College Theatre, 10. Mills College, 500 MacArthur Blvd, Oakland ☎ 430-3308

Paramount Theatre, 9. 2025 Broadway, Oakland ☎ 465-6400

Zellerbach Playhouse, 6. UC Berkeley ☎ 642-9988

SOUTH BAY

Burgess Theater, 12. 601 Laurel St, Menlo Park ☎ 650/323-9365

Mountain View Center for the Performing Arts, 11. Castro & Mercy Sts, Mountain View ☎ 650/903-6000

Villa Montalvo Center for the Arts, 13. 15400 Montalvo Rd, Saratoga ☎ 408/961-5800

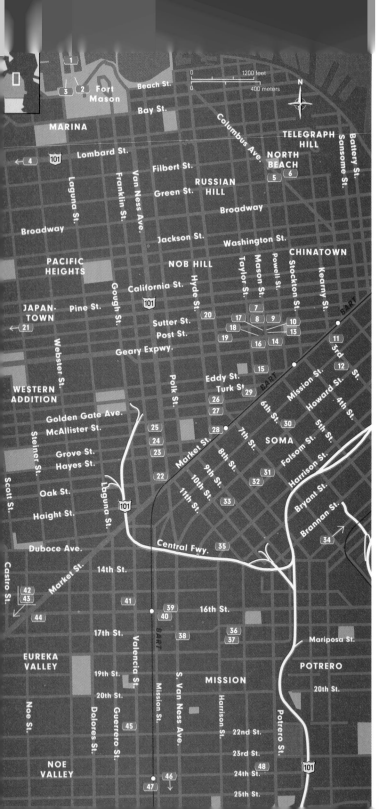

MAP 50

MAP **50** **Performing Arts/Downtown**

Listed Alphabetically (cont.)

Lorraine Hansberry Theatre, 7.
620 Sutter St ☎ 474-8800

Magic Theatre, 2.
Bldg D, Fort Mason ☎ 441-8822

Marines' Memorial Theatre, 8.
609 Sutter St ☎ 771-6900

The Marsh, 45.
1062 Valencia St ☎ 641-0235

Mason Street Theatre, 14.
340 Mason St ☎ 982-5463

Mission Cultural Center/El Teatro de la Esperanza, 47.
2868 Mission St ☎ 821-1155

New Conservatory Theatre Center, 22.
25 Van Ness Ave ☎ 861-8972

New Performance Gallery, 38.
3153 17th St ☎ 863-9834

Noh Space, 37.
2840 Mariposa St ☎ 621-7978

Orpheum Theatre, 28.
1192 Market St ☎ 521-2000

Palace of Fine Arts, 4.
3301 Lyon St ☎ 567-6642

Plush Room, 20.
940 Sutter St ☎ 885-2800

Phoenix Theatre, 32.
301 8th St ☎ 621-4423

San Francisco Ballet, 24. *see* War Memorial & Performing Arts Center

San Francisco Chamber Symphony, 11. 5 3rd St ☎ 495-2919

San Francisco Opera, 24. *see* War Memorial & Performing Arts Center

San Francisco Symphony, 23. *see* War Memorial & Performing Arts Center

Stage Door Theater, 13.
420 Mason St ☎ 249-0833

Studio Theatre, 43. San Francisco State University, 1600 Holloway Ave ☎ 338-2467

Theatre Artaud, 36.
450 Florida St ☎ 621-7797

Theatre Forte, 26.
220 Golden Gate Ave ☎ 882-1199

Theatre On The Square, 9.
450 Post St ☎ 433-9500

Theatre Rhinoceros, 39.
2926 16th St ☎ 861-5079

Victoria Theatre, 40.
2961 16th St ☎ 863-7576

War Memorial Opera House, 24.
see War Memorial & Performing Arts Center

WAR MEMORIAL & PERFORMING ARTS CENTER
Van Ness Ave-McAllister to Hayes Sts

Herbst Theatre, 25. 401 Van Ness Ave ☎ 392-4400

Louise M Davies Symphony Hall, 23. 201 Van Ness Ave ☎ 431-5400
San Francisco Symphony ☎ 864-6000

War Memorial Opera House, 24.
301 Van Ness Ave ☎ 864-6000
San Francisco Opera ☎ 864-3330
San Francisco Ballet ☎ 865-2000

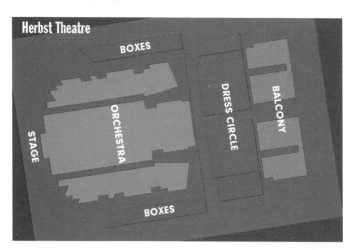

Herbst Theatre

Theaters/War Memorial Complex

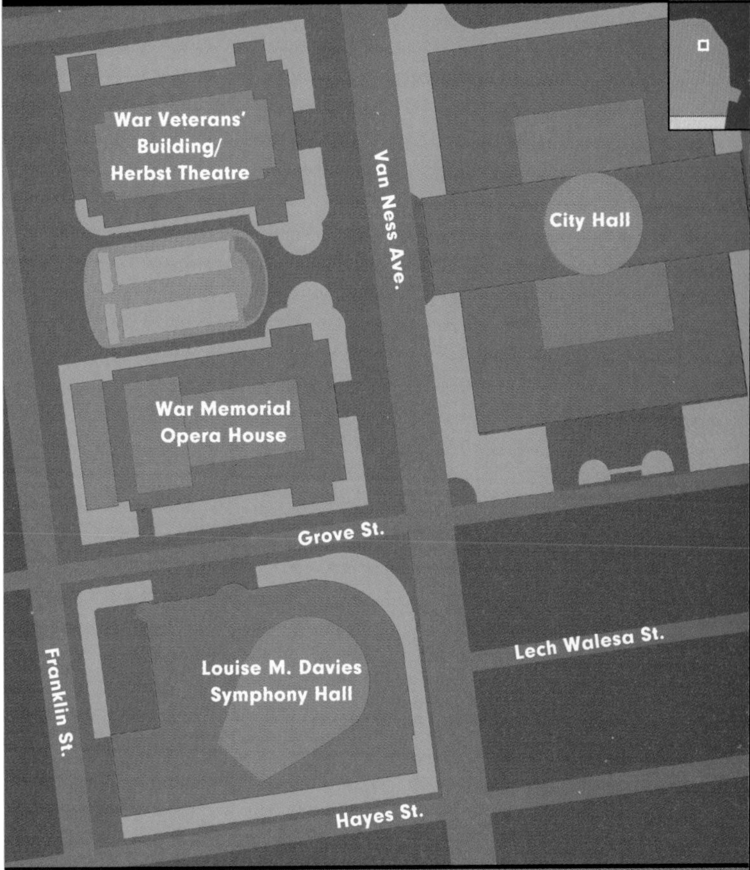
War Veterans' Building/ Herbst Theatre
Van Ness Ave.
City Hall
War Memorial Opera House
Grove St.
Lech Walesa St.
Franklin St.
Louise M. Davies Symphony Hall
Hayes St.

Opera House

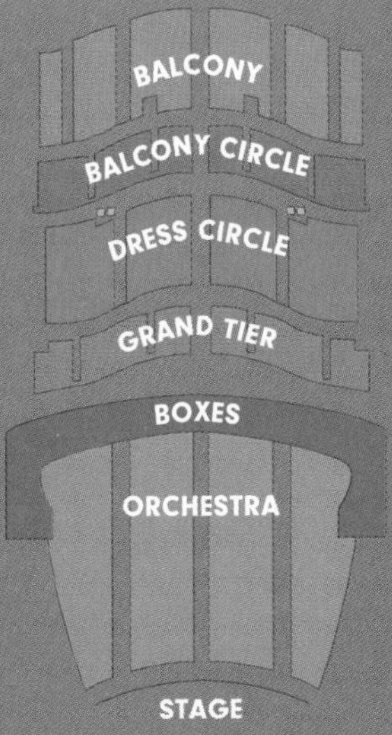
BALCONY
BALCONY CIRCLE
DRESS CIRCLE
GRAND TIER
BOXES
ORCHESTRA
STAGE

Symphony Hall

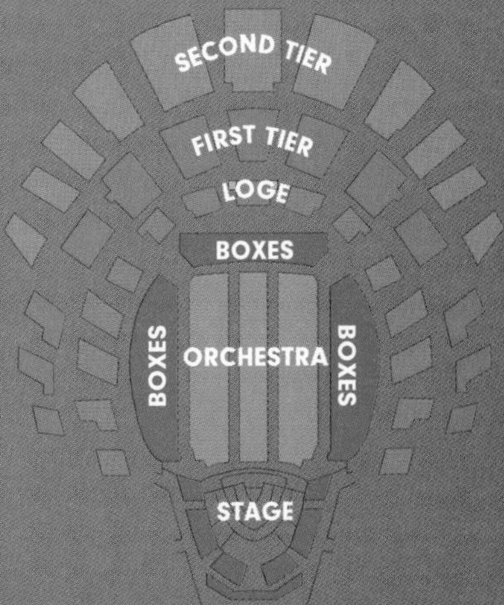
SECOND TIER
FIRST TIER
LOGE
BOXES
BOXES
ORCHESTRA
BOXES
STAGE

MAP 52 · Nightlife/SoMa & Downtown

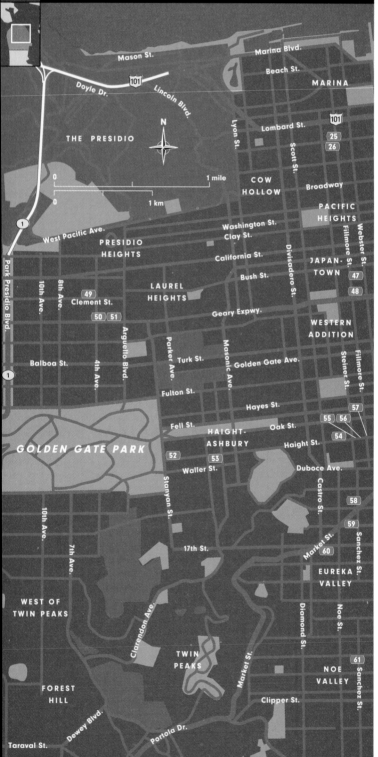

MAP **52**

Beach St.
30
29
Columbus Ave.
Bay St.
28
Lombard St.
TELEGRAPH
HILL
32
Sansome St.
Battery St.
NORTH
BEACH
31
Van Ness Ave.
Franklin St.
Polk St.
Larkin St.
RUSSIAN
HILL
33 34
35
36
Broadway
27
37
Jackson St.
Washington St.
CHINATOWN
38
BART
Clay St.
NOB HILL
Powell St.
Kearny St.
39
40
Main St.
1
Taylor St.
California St.
Market St.
2
Pine St.
101
Hyde St.
2nd St.
4
3
Bush St.
Gough St.
42
Geary St.
45
1st St.
80
43
O'Farrell St.
3rd St.
5
6
41
Mission St.
Folsom St.
Harrison St.
7
Laguna St.
44
Turk St.
46
Howard St.
4th St.
Golden Gate Ave.
6th St.
5th St.
8
Market St.
12
Grove St.
SOMA
13
Brannan St.
Webster St.
8th St.
11
10
101
9th St.
15
9
10th St.
16
Townsend St.
17
Bryant St.
14
18
7th St.
21
20
22
19
Central Fwy.
70
23
24
280
14th St.
15th St.
16th St.
69
S. Van Ness Ave.
16th St.
67
Mariposa St.
68
17th St.
66
BART
POTRERO
18th St.
Mission St.
20th St.
Missouri St.
CALTRAIN
19th St.
MISSION
Indiana St.
20th St.
21st St.
Harrison St.
Dolores St.
Guerrero St.
Valencia St.
64 65
22nd St.
Potrero St.
23rd St.
3rd St.
24th St.
25th St.
101
Army St.
Army St.
Mission St.
63
62
BAY
VIEW

MAP 52 Nightlife/SoMa & Downtown

Listed by Site Number

SOMA
1 Harry Denton's
2 Gordon Biersch
3 El Roys
4 DV8
5 Thirstybear Brewing Co.
6 The Sound Factory
7 Infusion
8 Club Townsend
9 The Trocadero
10 Hotel Utah
11 The Endup
12 Covered Wagon Saloon
13 1015 Folsom
14 Cafe Mars
15 Julie's Supper Club
16 Up & Down Club
17 Cat's Grill & Alley Club
18 The Stud
19 DNA Lounge
20 Slim's
21 Paradise Lounge
22 The Holy Cow
23 20 Tank Brewery
24 Eleven

EVERYWHERE ELSE
25 Pierce Street Annex
26 Balboa Cafe
27 Johnny Love's
28 Bimbo's 365 Club
29 Cobb's Comedy Club
30 Lou's Pier 47
31 Savoy-Tivoli
32 Pier 23 Cafe
33 Pearl's Jazz Restaurant & Bar
34 Spec's
35 Tosca Cafe
36 Vesuvio
37 The Punch Line
38 Sol y Luna
39 The Tonga Room
40 Top of The Mark
41 Mason Street Wine Bar
42 Edinburgh Castle
43 Great American Music Hall
44 Miss Pearl's Jam House
45 Club 181
46 The Warfield
47 Jack's Bar

48 The Fillmore
49 Last Day Saloon
50 Ireland's 32
51 Pat O'Shea's Mad Hatter
52 Club Boomerang
53 The DeLuxe
54 An Bodrán
55 Mad Dog in the Fog
56 Café International
57 Nickie's Barbeque
58 Café du Nord
59 The Café
60 Twin Peaks
61 Noe Valley Ministry
62 Cesar's Latin Palace
63 El Río
64 Lone Palm
65 Latin American Club
66 Elbo Room
67 The Rite Spot
68 Bottom of the Hill
69 Kilowatt
70 The Orbit Room

Listed Alphabetically   *Area Code (415) unless otherwise noted.*

An Bodrán, 54. 668 Haight St
☎ 431-4724. Irish Pub/Irish Music & Dancing

Balboa Cafe, 26. 3199 Fillmore St
921-3944. Bar

Bimbo's 365 Club, 28. 1025 Columbus Ave ☎ 474-0365. Eclectic Live Music

Bottom of the Hill, 68. 1233 17th St
☎ 626-4455. Bar/Alternative Music

Café du Nord, 58. 2170 Market St
☎ 861-5016. Bar/Eclectic Music

Café International, 56. 508 Haight St
☎ 552-7390. Coffeehouse/Acoustic

Café Mars, 14. 798 Brannan St
☎ 621-6277. Bar

Cat's Grill & Alley Club, 17.
1190 Folsom St ☎ 431-3332.
Comedy/Dance Club/Bar

Cesar's Latin Palace, 62. 3140 Mission St ☎ 648-6611. Latin Music/Dancing

Club Boomerang, 52. 1840 Haight St
☎ 387-2996. Alternative Music

Club 181, 45. 181 Eddy St ☎ 673-8181.
Live Jazz/Acid Jazz/Dance Club

Club Townsend, 8. 177 Townsend St
☎ 974-1156. Dance Club

Cobb's Comedy Club, 29. 2801
Leavenworth St ☎ 928-4320. Comedy

Covered Wagon Saloon, 12. 911
Folsom St ☎ 974-1585. Bar/Local Bands

The DeLuxe, 53. 1511 Haight St
☎ 552-6949. Bar/Swing Music

DNA Lounge, 19. 375 11th St
☎ 626-1409. Live Eclectic Music

DV8, 4. 55 Natoma St ☎ 957-1730.
Techno Dance Club

Edinburgh Castle, 42. 950 Geary St
☎ 885-4074. British Pub

El Río, 63. 3158 Mission St
☎ 282-3325. Bar/Salsa Music

MAP **52**

Listed Alphabetically (cont.)

El Roys, 3. 300 Beale St ☎ 882-7989. Bar/Beer Garden

Elbo Room, 66. 647 Valencia St ☎ 552-7788. Bar/Live Jazz/Funk

Eleven, 24. 374 11th St ☎ 431-3337. Bar/Live Jazz

The Endup, 11. 995 Harrison St ☎ 357-0827. Gay/Lesbian Dance Club

The Fillmore, 48. 1805 Geary St ☎ 346-6000. Live Alternative

Gordon Biersch, 2. 2 Harrison St ☎ 243-8246. Brewery Pub

Great American Music Hall, 42. 859 O'Farrell St ☎ 885-0750. Live Alternative

The Holy Cow, 22. 1535 Folsom St ☎ 621-6087. Top-40 Dance Club

Harry Denton's, 1. 161 Steuart St ☎ 882-1333. Bar/Live Music

Hotel Utah, 10. 500 4th St ☎ 421-8308. Bar/Local Bands

Infusion, 7. 555 2nd St ☎ 543-2282. Bar/Live Music

Ireland's 32, 50. 3920 Geary Blvd ☎ 386-6173. Irish Bar/Live Music

Jack's Bar, 47. 1601 Fillmore St ☎ 567-3227. Live Blues

Johnny Love's, 27. 1500 Broadway ☎ 931-8021. Bar

Julie's Supper Club, 15. 1123 Folsom St ☎ 861-0707. Supper Club

Kilowatt, 69. 3160 16th St ☎ 861-2595. Live Alternative

Last Day Saloon, 49. 406 Clement St ☎ 387-6343. Local Bands

Latin American Club, 65. 3286 22nd St ☎ 647-2732. Bar

Lone Palm, 64. 3394 22nd St ☎ 648-0109. Bar/Live Blues & Jazz

Lou's Pier 47, 30. 300 Jefferson St ☎ 771-0377. Jazz/R&B

Mad Dog in the Fog, 55. 530 Haight St ☎ 626-7279. British Pub

Mason Street Wine Bar, 41. 342 Mason St ☎ 391-3454. Live Jazz

Miss Pearl's Jam House, 44. 601 Eddy St ☎ 775-5267. DJ/Live Caribbean/Reggae

Nickie's Barbeque, 57. 460 Haight St ☎ 621-6508. Dance Music/Bar

Noe Valley Ministry, 61. 1021 Sanchez St ☎ 282-2317. Live Jazz/ Blues/Acoustic

1015 Folsom, 13. 1015 Folsom St ☎ 431-1200. Dance Club

The Orbit Room, 70. 1900 Market St ☎ 252-9525. Bar

Paradise Lounge, 21. 1501 Folsom St ☎ 861-6906. Bar/Live Music

Pat O'Shea's Mad Hatter, 51. 3848 Geary Blvd ☎ 752-3148. Irish Pub

Pearl's Jazz Restaurant & Bar, 33. 256 Columbus Ave ☎ 291-8255. Jazz

Pier 23 Cafe, 32. The Embarcadero ☎ 362-5125. Bar/Live Jazz

Pierce Street Annex, 25. 3138 Fillmore St ☎ 567-1400. Bar

The Punch Line, 37. 444 Battery St ☎ 397-7573. Comedy

The Rite Spot, 67. 2099 Folsom St ☎ 552-6066. Bar

Savoy-Tivoli, 31. 1434 Grant Ave ☎ 362-7023. Bar

Slim's, 20. 333 11th St ☎ 255-0333. Live Pop/Alternative

Sol y Luna, 38. 475 Sacramento St ☎ 296-8191. Supper Club/Latin

The Sound Factory, 6. 525 Harrison St ☎ 243-9646. Disco

Spec's, 34. 12 Adler Pl ☎ 421-4112. Bar

The Stud, 18. 399 9th St ☎ 252-7883. Bar/Gay

The Café, 59. 2367 Market St ☎ 861-3846. Bar/Gay & Lesbian

Thirstybear Brewing Co., 5. 661 Howard St ☎ 974-0905. Microbrewery

Top of The Mark, 40. Mark Hopkins Hotel, 999 California St ☎ 392-3434. Bar

The Tonga Room, 39. Fairmont Hotel, 950 Mason St ☎ 772-5278. Cocktail Lounge

Tosca Cafe, 35. 242 Columbus Ave ☎ 391-1244. Bar/Cafe

The Trocadero, 9. 520 4th St ☎ 495-6620. Music/Dancing

20 Tank Brewery, 23. 316 11th St ☎ 255-9455. Microbrewery

Twin Peaks, 60. 401 Castro St ☎ 864-9470. Bar/Gay

Up & Down Club, 16. 1151 Folsom St ☎ 626-2388. Live Jazz/DJ Dancing

Vesuvio, 36. 255 Columbus Ave ☎ 362-3370. Bar

The Warfield, 46. 982 Market St ☎ 775-7722. Live Rock

MAP 53 Nightlife/East Bay

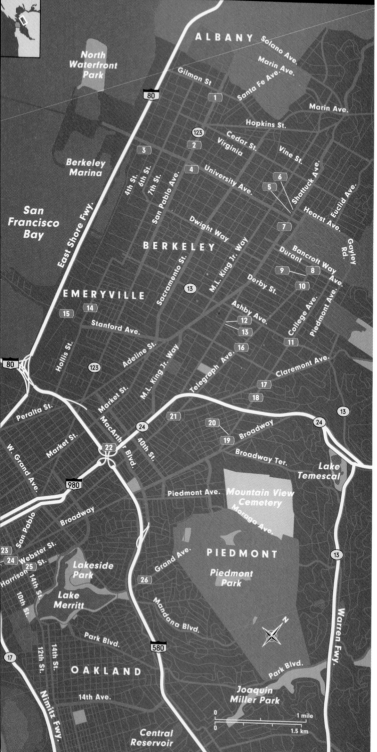

MAP 53

Listed by Site Number

1 Ashkenaz
2 The Albatross
3 Brennan's
4 Freight and Salvage Coffee House
5 Spats
6 Triple Rock Brewery
7 Jupiter
8 Blake's
9 Raleigh's
10 Bison Brewing Co
11 Espresso Roma
12 Starry Plough
13 La Peña Cultural Center
14 Chalkers Billiard Club
15 Kimball's East
16 The White Horse Inn
17 The Graduate
18 Barclay's
19 McNally's Irish Pub
20 George and Walt's
21 The Bird Kage
22 Eli's Mile High
23 Pacific Coast Brewing Company
24 Yoshi's
25 Caribee Dance Center
26 The Alley

Listed Alphabetically   Area Code (510) unless otherwise noted.

The Albatross, 2.
1822 San Pablo Ave, Berkeley
☎ 843-2473. Bar

The Alley, 26. 3325 Grand Ave, Oakland ☎ 444-8505. Bar

Ashkenaz, 1. 1317 San Pablo Ave, Berkeley ☎ 525-5054.
World Music, Dancing

Barclay's, 18. 5940 College Ave, Oakland ☎ 654-1650. Bar

The Bird Kage, 21.
4822 Telegraph Ave, Oakland
☎ 655-0300. Bar/Jazz

Bison Brewing Co, 10.
2598 Telegraph Ave, Berkeley
☎ 841-7734. Microbrewery/ Live Music

Blake's, 8. 2367 Telegraph Ave, Berkeley
☎ 848-0886. Bar/Blues

Brennan's, 3. 720 University Ave, Berkeley
☎ 841-0960. Irish Pub

Caribee Dance Center, 25. 1408 Webster St, Oakland ☎ 835-4006.
Dance Club

Chalkers Billiard Club, 14.
5900 Hollis St, Emeryville
☎ 658-5821. Pool

Eli's Mile High, 22.
3629 Martin Luther King Jr Way, Oakland
☎ 655-6661. Bar/Blues

Espresso Roma, 11.
2960 College Ave, Berkeley
☎ 644-3773. Coffeehouse

Freight and Salvage Coffee House, 4. 1111 Addison St, Berkeley
☎ 548-1761. Alternative Music

George and Walt's, 20.
5445 College Ave, Oakland
☎ 653-7441. Bar

The Graduate, 17. College & Claremont Aves, Oakland
☎ 655-8847. Bar/Gay

Jupiter, 7. 2181 Shattuck Ave, Berkeley
☎ 843-8277. Microbrewery/Acoustic

Kimball's East, 15.
5800 Shellmound St, Emeryville
☎ 658-2555. Jazz/Pop

La Peña Cultural Center, 13.
3105 Shattuck Ave, Berkeley
☎ 849-2568. Latin-American Music/Dance

McNally's Irish Pub, 19.
5352 College Ave, Oakland
☎ 654-9463. Irish Pub

Pacific Coast Brewing Company, 23.
906 Washington St, Oakland
☎ 836-2739. Microbrewery

Raleigh's, 9. 2438 Telegraph Ave, Berkeley ☎ 848-8652. Bar

Spats, 5. 1974 Shattuck Ave, Berkeley
☎ 841-7225. Cocktail Lounge

Starry Plough, 12. 3101 Shattuck Ave, Berkeley ☎ 841-2082.
Bar/Acoustic/Irish

Triple Rock Brewery, 6.
1920 Shattuck Ave, Berkeley
☎ 843-2739. Microbrewery

The White Horse Inn, 16.
6551 Telegraph Ave, Oakland
☎ 652-3820. Bar/Gay/Lesbian

Yoshi's, 24. 510 Embarcadero West, Oakland ☎ 238-9200. Jazz/Blues

MAP **54** **Movies/Bay Area**

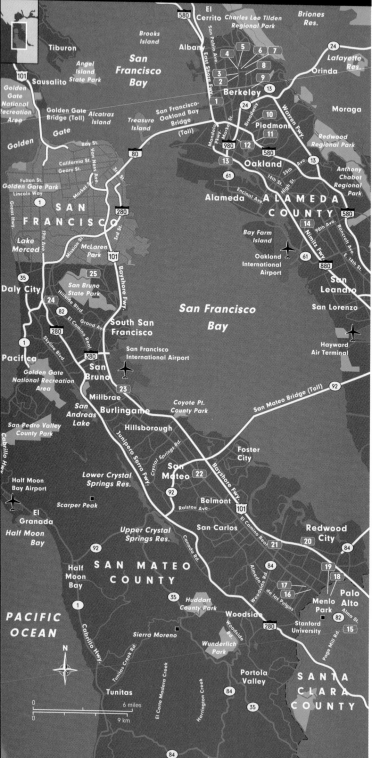

MAP 55 Movies/San Francisco

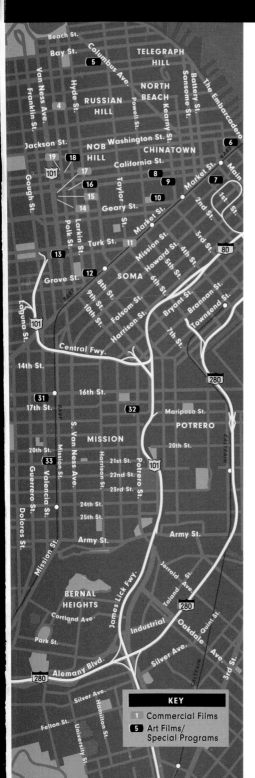

MAP **55**

Listed by
Site Number

Presidio
2 Cinema 21
3 United Artists
Metro
4 Alhambra
5 SF Art Institute
6 Embarcadero
Center Cinema
7 Japan Information
Center
8 Goethe Institut
9 Istituto Italiano di
Cultura
10 Bomani Gallery
11 St Francis Theaters
12 San Francisco Public
Library
13 Opera Plaza
Cinemas
14 United Artists
Galaxy
15 Regency II
16 Alliance Francaise
17 Regency I
18 Lumiere 3
19 Royal
20 Clay
21 AMC Kabuki 8
Theatres
22 United Artists Vogue
23 Bridge
24 United Artists
Coronet
25 United Artists
Alexandria
26 Four Star
27 Balboa
28 The Red Vic
29 UCSF Cole Hall
Cinema
30 Castro
31 The Roxie
32 San Francisco
Cinematheque
33 Artists' Television
Access
34 Noe Valley Branch
Gallery
35 Empire Cinema
36 United Irish Cultural
Center
37 United Artists
Stonestown Twin

MAP **55** **Movies/San Francisco**

Listed Alphabetically   Area Code (415) unless otherwise noted.

COMMERCIAL FILMS

Alhambra, 4. 2330 Polk St
☎ 775-2137

AMC Kabuki 8 Theatres, 21.
1881 Post St
☎ 931-9800

Balboa, 27. 3630 Balboa St
☎ 221-8184

Cinema 21, 2. 2141 Chestnut St
☎ 921-6720

Embarcadero Center Cinema, 6.
1 Embarcadero Center ☎ 352-0810

Empire Cinema, 35. 85 West Portal
Ave ☎ 661-2539

Presidio, 1. 2340 Chestnut St
☎ 922-1318

Regency I, 17.
1320 Van Ness Ave at Sutter St
☎ 885-6773

Regency II, 15.
1268 Sutter St at Van Ness Ave
☎ 776-8054

Royal, 19. 1529 Polk St
☎ 474-0353

St Francis Theaters, 11. 965 Market St
☎ 362-4822

United Artists Alexandria, 25.
5400 Geary Blvd
☎ 752-5100

United Artists Coronet, 24.
3575 Geary Blvd
☎ 752-4400

United Artists Galaxy, 14.
1285 Sutter St
☎ 474-8700

United Artists Metro, 3.
2055 Union St
☎ 931-1685

United Artists Stonestown Twin, 37.
501 Buckingham Way
☎ 221-8182

Clay, 20. 2261 Fillmore St
☎ 352-0810

Four Star, 26. 2200 Clement St
☎ 666-3488

Goethe Institut, 8. 530 Bush St
☎ 391-0370

Istituto Italiano di Cultura, 9.
425 Bush St
☎ 788-7142

Japan Information Center, 7.
50 Fremont St
☎ 356-2464

Lumiere 3, 18. 1572 California St
☎ 352-0810

Noe Valley Branch Library, 34.
451 Jersey St
☎ 695-5095

Opera Plaza Cinemas, 13.
601 Van Ness Ave
☎ 352-0810

The Red Vic, 28. 1727 Haight St
☎ 668-3994

The Roxie, 31. 3117 16th St
☎ 863-1087

SF Art Institute, 5. 800 Chestnut St
☎ 749-4545

SF Cinematheque, 32. 480 Potrero
Ave ☎ 558-8129

SF Public Library, 12.
Larkin & Grove Sts ☎ 557-4400

United Artists Vogue, 22.
3290 Sacramento St
☎ 221-8183

United Irish Cultural Center, 36.
2700 45th Ave
☎ 661-2700

UCSF Cole Hall Cinema, 29.
513 Parnassus Ave
☎ 476-2542

ART FILMS/SPECIAL PROGRAMS

Alliance Francaise, 16. 1345 Bush St
☎ 775-7755

Artists' Television Access, 33.
992 Valencia St
☎ 824-3890

Bomani Gallery, 10. 251 Post St
☎ 296-8677

Bridge, 23. 3010 Geary Blvd
☎ 751-3212

Castro, 30. 429 Castro St
☎ 621-6120